LECTIO DIVINA
—the sacred art—

Transforming Words & Images into Heart-Centered Prayer

Christine Valters Paintner

Walking Together, Finding the Way®
SKYLIGHT PATHS®
PUBLISHING
Woodstock, Vermont

Lectio Divina—*The Sacred Art:*
Transforming Words and Images into Heart-Centered Prayer
2011 Quality Paperback Edition, First Printing
© 2011 by Christine Valters Paintner

For information regarding permission to reprint material from this book, please write or fax your request to SkyLight Paths Publishing, Permissions Department, at the address / fax number listed below, or e-mail your request to permissions@skylightpaths.com.

Grateful acknowledgment is given for permission to use the following: Contributions throughout from Roxanne Morgan, Edith O'Nuallain, Deb Swingholm, Cheryl Macpherson, Sally Brower, Cathy Johnson, Laurie Kathleen Clark, Eveline Maedel, Judy Smoot, Sharon Richards, Eileen Downard, © by the authors; p. 151, icon by Heather Williams Durka, © by the artist; p. 197, mandala by Stacy Wills, www.stacywills.com, © by the artist.

Unless otherwise indicated, Scripture quotations are from the *New Revised Standard Version Bible*, copyright © 1989 by the Division of Christian Education of the National Council of the Churches of Christ in the USA. Used by permission. All rights reserved.

Library of Congress Cataloging-in-Publication Data
Paintner, Christine Valters.
Lectio divina—the sacred art : transforming words and images into heart-centered prayer / Christine Valters Paintner. — Quality paperback ed.
p. cm.
Includes bibliographical references (p.   ) and index.
ISBN 978-1-59473-300-0 (quality pbk. original : alk. paper) 1. Spiritual life—Christianity. 2. Spiritual life. 3. Prayer—Christianity. 4. Prayer. 5. Bible—Devotional use. 6. Sacred books—Devotional use. 7. Christianity and other religions. I. Title.
BV4501.3.P336 2011
248.3—dc22
2011013926
10 9 8 7 6 5 4 3 2 1
Manufactured in the United States of America
Cover Design: Jenny Buono

SkyLight Paths Publishing is creating a place where people of different spiritual traditions come together for challenge and inspiration, a place where we can help each other understand the mystery that lies at the heart of our existence.

SkyLight Paths sees both believers and seekers as a community that increasingly transcends traditional boundaries of religion and denomination—people wanting to learn from each other, *walking together, finding the way.*

SkyLight Paths, "Walking Together, Finding the Way," and colophon are trademarks of LongHill Partners, Inc., registered in the U.S. Patent and Trademark Office.

Walking Together, Finding the Way®
Published by SkyLight Paths Publishing
A Division of LongHill Partners, Inc.
Sunset Farm Offices, Route 4, P.O. Box 237
Woodstock, VT 05091
Tel: (802) 457-4000 Fax: (802) 457-4004
www.skylightpaths.com

To my beloved:
Your love for me is a sacred text
shimmering with God's beauty.

CONTENTS

PART TWO
THE FOUR MOVEMENTS OF *LECTIO DIVINA*

INTRODUCTION

They can be like a sun, words.
They can do for the heart
what light can
for a field.
        —*John of the Cross,* Love Poems from God

In October 2009 I was on pilgrimage in Ireland. We were visiting Glendalough, the ruins of an ancient Celtic monastic community founded by St. Kevin. One morning was dark and stormy, and I had taken a long walk on the property and was watching the great gatherings of crows in the trees. Suddenly the clouds rolled apart and the sun spilled her illumination across the wet field in front of me. The moment of that sweeping of light, unfolding across the green grass, was a transcendent one. My heart quickened, my breathing grew deep and slow, my imagination felt expansive. When I later found this poem by John of the Cross, this moment came rushing back to me. *Lectio divina* is like that; we can sit with a sacred text in the dark fields of the mind, and suddenly by grace, we have a moment of illumination. Our hearts feel radiant as we have an encounter with the Holy One through the sacred words. In that moment in Ireland there were beautiful, gentle cows in the field, slowly chewing their cud. The ancient monks would look at cows and see in them a metaphor for the tasting, chewing, savoring, and digesting of Scripture. The process of praying *lectio divina* means we delight in the nourishment sacred texts offer to us and integrate their wisdom into our lives.

In ancient times, wise men and women fled out into the desert to find a place where they could be fully present to God and to their own inner struggles at work within them. They sought out radical silence, solitude, and continuous prayer, becoming known as the desert mothers and fathers, the earliest Christian monks and hermits. The desert became a place to enter into the refiner's fire and be stripped down to your holy essence. The desert was a threshold place from which you emerged a different person. Many people followed these *ammas* and *abbas,* mothers and fathers, seeking their wisdom and guidance for a meaningful life. One tradition was to ask them for a word—this word or phrase would be something on which to chew, ponder, meditate, and engage with holy curiosity for many days, weeks, months, or sometimes a whole lifetime. This practice is one of the roots of *lectio divina*, where we approach the sacred texts with the same request. "Give me a word," we ask the scriptures—something to nourish me, challenge me, a word I can wrestle with and grow into, something to transform my heart.

Lectio divina essentially means "divine reading." When we read a sacred text we enter into an encounter with God. For the purpose of this book, "sacred text" can refer to the scriptures of different religious traditions, such as the Hebrew and Christian scriptures and the Qur'an. However, I will also be inviting you to expand your sense of what a sacred text might be as you learn to encounter the Divine Presence through poetry, art, music, nature, and your life story.

Pause for a moment now as you begin this journey into an ancient practice. Reflect on a time when you were given a word or phrase—perhaps from Scripture, perhaps a jewel of wisdom from the lips of someone who loves you, perhaps from a book that transformed your life in unexpected ways. Savor this moment, simply honoring the grace and gift received and allowing your heart to fill with anticipation for the next word that will invite you into a heart-centered change.

Words can illuminate our hearts; they contain the seeds of invitation to cross a new threshold. Words ripen within us. We can receive a word and not realize its full impact for our lives for a long while, until one day we suddenly see things differently. I often find lines of poems singing in my heart for months after they have spoken to me, inviting me deeper into their wisdom. *Lectio divina* is an ancient practice of listening deeply to the voice of God speaking through these sacred texts. *Lectio* cultivates in us the ability to be fully present to the holy call that emerges from words.

THE GIFTS OF *LECTIO DIVINA*

When I first discovered *lectio divina* several years ago I fell in love with the practice for many reasons:

- The rhythm of *lectio*'s four movements reflect the natural opening of the spirit in prayer
- The foundational belief of *lectio* that God speaks through the sacred texts in unique ways to each one of us at each particular moment of our lives
- The cultivation through *lectio* of our capacity to listen deeply for God in the whole of life.

Lectio divina is a practice of being present to each moment in a heart-centered way. We are often taught in religious communities to think through our prayers—reciting words and formulas that are valuable elements of our shared traditions, but only one window into God's presence. In *lectio* we invite God to speak to us in an unmediated way. Our memories, images, and feelings become an important context for experiencing God's voice active in us, and we discover it when we pray from our hearts. Those words moving through us break open God's invitation to us in this moment of our lives and call us to respond.

I am a Benedictine oblate, which means that I have made a commitment to a particular monastic community—St. Placid Priory in Lacey, Washington—to live out monastic spirituality in my everyday life as a layperson and writer, artist, teacher, and spiritual director. At home with my husband, in the heart of Seattle, I am called to live in a slow, mindful, and intentional way in the midst of all the demands of daily life like grocery shopping, walking the dog, balancing my checkbook, going on dates with my husband, spending time with friends, and working each day to make ends meet. I am even called to this path when illness and grief trouble our family, or when I read of some heartbreak around the world. Some days are easier than others, but it is my commitment to the practice that is important. *Lectio divina* offers me a way to greet each moment with full presence and discover the Sacred there.

I first discovered *lectio divina* during my doctoral studies in Christian spirituality at the Graduate Theological Union. As I studied more about monastic tradition and the Rule of Benedict, a monastic code and guide for daily life in the monasteries of the West, I discovered a rich and ancient tradition with practices that support contemplative ways of being in the world. In *lectio divina*, I found a compelling and beautiful way to move my prayer deeper and began intuitively to incorporate the practice into my teaching and retreat work, as a way to pray with Scripture as well as art, music, poetry, dreams, nature, and life experience. From this beginning I fell in love with all the dimensions of Benedictine life—the rhythm of praying at fixed times each day, entering into silence through centering prayer, the commitment to hospitality and humility—and my call was to bring these to the everyday world beyond the walls of the cloister. I believe we all have an inner contemplative dimension; I like to call this my "inner monk." This part of me longs for hours of silence and the gift of simply being, rather than doing. In monastic tradition I found a path that supports the flowering of my inner monk in ways other paths had not.

In my work as a teacher, retreat leader, and writer, my areas of specialization are monastic spirituality, with a love of desert, Celtic, and Benedictine traditions. I bring the practice of *lectio divina* to almost anything I am teaching, and I have co-authored a previous book on *lectio* geared primarily toward a Catholic audience. In this book I hope to reach an even wider audience of people interested in this form of contemplative prayer. I also want to expand the application of *lectio* beyond traditional religious texts to other places and experiences where we encounter the Holy. This book is written for those beginning to explore contemplative prayer, Christians who are looking for new ways to approach their *lectio divina* practice, and those outside the Christian tradition who want to explore some of the contemplative riches from Western spirituality.

THE STRUCTURE OF THIS BOOK

Part One of this book is an introduction to some of the foundations for a practice of *lectio divina*. Chapter One explores *lectio* as a practice of sacred reading within the context of other spiritual and religious traditions that honor the way God's voice speaks through words and text, while Chapter Two looks at the tradition of heart-centered prayer as a dominant metaphor throughout the Hebrew and Christian scriptures and the foundation of *lectio divina*. St. Benedict begins his rule by inviting us to "listen with the ear of our heart," and this is the central movement of *lectio divina*: to encounter God in the center of our own beings. Thus Chapter Three examines the three central Benedictine values of stability, obedience, and conversion, what these might mean for our contemporary lives, and how they support contemplative prayer. In

Chapter Four we look at what a sacred text is and how to choose one for this practice.

Part Two explores each of the four movements of *lectio divina*. Chapter Five breaks open the first movement of *lectio*, which is to settle into a prayerful space, read the sacred text, and listen for a word or phrase that calls out to you—what I describe as "shimmers"—and then spend a few moments gently repeating it. The monastic practice of simplicity helps us release what hinders us from entering into prayer. Chapter Six examines the second movement, which is reflection, allowing the word or phrase to unfold in your imagination, listening for what images, feelings, and memories are stirring and then savoring the experience. It uses the Benedictine practice of inner hospitality as a way of welcoming in what stirs. In Chapter Seven we look at the third movement of *lectio*, which involves responding to what has been stirring within us and listening for the invitation from God. It may be a summons toward a new awareness or action, something that ultimately is in service to others and to your community. This chapter explores this movement of call and response, connecting it to the Benedictine practice of humility. Chapter Eight explores the fourth movement—slowing down even more and resting in the presence of God, simply being. This is an invitation to the stillness of contemplative prayer and is rooted in monastic practices of silence and solitude. One of the fruits of contemplation is a deepened sense of gratitude.

In Part Three, I invite you to expand your practice of *lectio* beyond scriptural texts to a sacred reading of the world. The four movements of *lectio* offer a rhythm that will cultivate your ability to experience God's presence in the world around you. Chapter Nine looks at *visio divina,* or sacred seeing, which applies these principles of sacred reading to praying visually with art, and explores the way different religious traditions invite us into praying with our eyes. Chapter Ten explores music as another sacred text through which we can encounter the Holy, pointing out the way different religious traditions regard sound as a primordial experience. Chapter Eleven explores nature as a sacred text and place of revelation of the Holy, looking at the way different religious traditions regard creation as the dwelling place of God. Chapter Twelve considers our lives as a source of sacred texts and stories, including our life experience, dreams, and bodies.

The Afterword invites you to consider the ways your life might be transformed through the gifts of reading the world in this way, and the appendices offer invitations and suggestions for praying *lectio* in a small group setting and on retreat. I also include suggestions for further reading.

Each chapter also includes specific practices for deepening your prayer and suggested texts for *lectio divina*—from Christian, Jewish, and other wisdom traditions—but you are welcome to use any text you like. The practices I suggest help break open the different movements of *lectio divina* for a deeper understanding of the whole process. I recommend reading the book through in order because the chapters build upon one another. Allow it to be an experience of slowly savoring the gifts *lectio* has to offer to your heart and spirit. I invite you to join me on a journey into the wisdom of an ancient practice that cultivates in us the capacity to tend to the sacred stirrings in all moments of our lives.

Lectio divina is not an analytic or a linear practice, but a practice of the heart that brings integration and meaning to our lives. We live in a culture that values efficiency and rationality over other kinds of gifts and wisdom, so the explorations through art and poetry I suggest are meant as ways to honor the intuitive aspects of your prayer and give them form and expression. My background is in the expressive arts, which engages creativity for healing and transformation. You can certainly gain value from the experience of simply praying *lectio* in its traditional form. I invite you, however, if you are at all curious, to open yourself up to some playful exploration through the gifts of poetry and art-making as well. The focus in this way of creating is on process over product; making art can become a part of the prayer experience and another way for God to speak and you to hear.

AN INVITATION TO EVERYONE

One of the most beautiful aspects of *lectio divina* for me is that although it developed within a Christian context as a way of praying with Scripture, the rhythms and movements of this practice are available to anyone. As we will explore in the third section, we can pray with a variety of sacred texts. No matter what tradition you come from, you can:

- Be present to your breath, move into your heart center, and read slowly.
- Savor the text and pay attention to feelings, images, and memories stirring.
- Listen for the way your life is being impacted by this experience and for an invitation arising from your new awareness in prayer.
- Release thoughts and images and rest into an experience of inner stillness.

This book is an offering of the heart. It is a deep honor to spend much of my precious time in this life breaking open the gifts of contemplative practices for everyone. I believe that all of us have within an "inner monk"—an aspect of ourselves that longs for silence and an encounter with the Holy Presence. Nurture your own inner monk in these pages. This book is meant to be read through slowly and practiced. Reading without practice simply gives us an intellectual understanding of a concept. Praying with the heart invites insight and transformation.

PART ONE

Beginning Our Exploration of *Lectio Divina*

SACRED READING

Listening for a Sacred Word

Give me a small line of verse from time to time, oh
   God,
and if I cannot write it down for lack of paper or
   light,
then let me address it softly in the evening to your
   Great Heaven.
But please give me a small line of verse.
                    —*Etty Hillesum*, An Interrupted Life

Lectio divina is an ancient Christian contemplative prayer practice enjoying a revival among laypeople. The Latin phrase literally means "divine reading." The use of the word *divine* implies
that the reading brings us to a kind of closeness with God's very
being rather than with a sacred object one step removed. The
word *lectio* is derived from the verb *legere*, which means "to
choose or pick." *Lectio divina* may be said to be "a divine picking
or choosing of a given sentence, phrase or word through which
God('s self) speaks. While certainly sacred (or *sacra*), one quickly
discovers that *lectio* appeals directly to the heart of God."[1] *Lectio
divina* is a contemplative way of praying with sacred texts where
we encounter God in a profoundly intimate and direct way.

THE DEVELOPMENT OF *LECTIO DIVINA* IN CHRISTIAN TRADITION

The ancient practice of *lectio divina* has its roots in Judaism. *Lectio divina* flows out of a Hebrew method of studying Scripture called *haggadah*, a process of learning by heart:

> *Haggadah* was an interactive interpretation of the Scriptures by means of the free use of the text to explore its inner meaning. It was part of the devotional practice of the Jews in the days of Jesus. The Jews would memorize the text in a process that involved repeating the passage over and over softly with the lips until the words themselves gradually took up residence in the heart, thereby transforming the person's life.[2]

The earliest forms of *lectio* as a Christian prayer method were practiced widely in the desert monastic tradition. In the third to fifth centuries, early Christians fled the cities to live in the spare and barren landscape of the desert of Egypt, Palestine, and Syria. There they lived an often austere life focused on prayer and presence to God, and many people sought them as wise guides and elders. The desert monks didn't have their own Bibles so they would memorize vast amounts of Scripture and in this way could meditate on the sacred texts throughout their day.

Saint Benedict of Nursia, who lived at the turn of the sixth century, is credited with promoting and refining its use. "Listen readily to holy reading, and devote yourself often to prayer," he writes in the Rule of Benedict. He also prescribes that sacred reading should occur during fixed hours of time and take place during special times of study. In addition, Benedict specifies that sacred reading should occur during meals and in community gatherings. During the Lenten season even more hours of the day are to be dedicated to this act of holy reading.

This was the more monastic style of *lectio divina* in which a monk might hear a word or phrase during the communal prayer of the Liturgy of the Hours and then hold it in his or her heart throughout the day. This process was described as "rumination," a gentle chewing of the word as a cow slowly chews cud. Eventually it would lead to inner movement, insight, and contemplation. While there are different qualities to these movements, the experience was more of an organic process of being led by the Spirit in prayer. It had a fluid and responsive quality to it.

Eventually a more scholastic form of *lectio divina* was created by a twelfth-century Carthusian monk named Guigo II. In his book *Ladder of Monks*, he breaks down the four movements into distinct parts, puts them in a systematic order, and analyzes them in connection with theological understandings, as was the practice of his time. He calls it "the ladder of four rungs by which we may well climb to heaven." His book is a classic in Western mysticism because it is considered to be the first description of systematic prayer and is still in use today.

In his book *Praying the Bible: Introduction to Lectio Divina*, Mariano Magrassi describes Scripture with a variety of moving images. It is like "a letter written to us by God to manifest his secrets, a mirror that reveals to us our inner face, a wheat field that nourishes the spirit, a priceless treasure."[3] Our spiritual ancestors regarded the sacred text as living because it is animated in an ongoing way by the Spirit. It was not written once to remain fossilized in its historical form, but the inspired words continue to reveal the wisdom of God's desires for us and our world at each moment in time.

SACRED READING IN OTHER TRADITIONS

Most religious traditions have a canon of texts that are regarded as sacred because of their ability to speak to us across the perceived barriers of time. This power of words and their living, vibrant quality, able to meet us in this moment of our lives, is the movement behind the practice of *lectio divina*. These texts are read in different ways than ordinary books. Judaism, Islam, and Buddhism, for example, each have reverential ways of reading that acknowledge and honor the fact that the voice of the Sacred speaks through these words.

In Judaism, the term *PaRDeS* means "paradise," "orchard," or "garden" in Hebrew, and is an acronym formed from the first letters of four words: *p'shat, remez, d'rash*, and *sud*. These four words represent four levels of meaning in traditional Jewish reading and exegesis of the Bible: *p'shat* refers to the literal meaning of the text, *remez* refers to the metaphorical or symbolic meaning, *d'rash* refers to the moral meaning or lesson, and *sud* refers to the deeper mystical meaning. Later, Christian monks and scholars appropriated this same system for reading sacred scriptures and referred to them as the literal, allegorical, moral, and mystical levels, which also correspond to the four movements of *lectio divina*.

In Islamic tradition, the holy text of the Qur'an is at the center of life and practice for Muslims. Its words are regarded as received by the prophet Muhammad through which God, the Creator of all, speaks directly to humanity:

> The revealed words of this Qur'an, when experienced reverently and profoundly, are not relics from the past but exist in a timeless present, communicating as vividly as when they were first uttered. If we are patient and concentrate, we will discover that these words of Allah often refer with mysterious precision to whatever historical or personal situation presents itself to us.
>
> The encounter with the Qur'an as living revelation is the single thread from which all the dimensions of Muslim spiritual life and civilization are woven.[4]

Christians believe that the Hebrew and Christian scriptures are also a "living revelation" with words that communicate to us in remarkable ways across time. It is precisely this aliveness of the sacred texts and wisdom that renders them rich food for prayer. In Hindu tradition, the sacred text of the Upanishads says: "The essence of man is speech. The essence of speech is sacred language. The essence of sacred language is word and sound. The essence of word and sound is Om." The word is considered to be the creative power that both sustains and destroys the cosmos:

> The Inspired schools of the Upanishads have developed
> an exalted teaching on sounds (*shabda*) and words which
> proceed from the eternal Word and through which one
> can enter into communion with it. The eternal Word itself
> is silent beyond silence.[5]

Out of this understanding arises the practice of repeating a mantra or sacred word. The word *mantra* literally means "an instrument of thought," a higher form of thought that leads to liberation and union.

In *Being Still: Reflections on an Ancient Mystical Tradition*, Jean-Yves Leloup writes that when we reflect on the similarities of other traditions to our own, "it is simply to recall the unity of humanity as such. The truth of one tradition ought to be found under its own proper forms and nuances in other traditions. Otherwise it would be an impoverished truth."[6] Reflecting on the tradition of sacred reading from other paths highlights the depth and richness of *lectio divina* as a spiritual practice and the universality of its movements.

CENTRAL ASSUMPTIONS OF *LECTIO DIVINA*

> *Your word is a lamp to my feet*
> *and a light to my path.*
>
> —*Psalm 119:105*

The practice of *lectio divina* is centered on some fundamental assumptions:

- The ancient desert fathers and mothers believed that the Hebrew and Christian scriptures were like a love letter written to us by God. They are living and animated in an ongoing way by the Spirit. The texts speak to us in this unique moment of our lives, wherever we find ourselves. Each time we come to the text we are in a new place and the text responds directly to what is happening in this moment. *Lectio* assumes that God speaks to us intimately in the unique circumstances of our lives, responding in new ways to each moment.

- The scriptures are an inexhaustible mystery that offer us an unending source of wisdom. Mariano Magrassi describes it this way: "It is infinite in extent, no reading can ever reach the bottom. The [ancients] love to use various images: it is a vast sea, an unfathomable abyss. Augustine speaks of 'an immense weight of mysteries,'... It is an exploration that will never end. No matter how much the mind reaches out and strives to understand, it can never encompass the full dimensions of a sacred text 'that spans infinite mysteries.'"[7]

- God is already praying in us. Through *lectio*, we make ourselves available to join this unceasing prayer already happening in our hearts. God is the one who initiates the dialogue. Our practice is to make space to hear this prayer already at work within us.

- *Lectio divina* is not about acquiring head knowledge of Scripture, but about a profound encounter with the heart of God. What is necessary for this prayer is a willingness to surrender yourself to the process. The thinking mind will try to control what unfolds, or analyze and judge what is happening. The heart is the place of receptivity, integration, and meaning-making. It is where thinking, feeling, intuition, and wisdom come together. In this process we are called to nothing short of transformation.

- When we pray *lectio divina* we see the words of Scripture as God's living words being spoken to our hearts in this moment. This approach to prayer is an encounter with a God who is active in and intimate with our lives. The primary action of this kind of prayer is listening for how God is already praying within us.

One of the things I value most about the practice of *lectio divina* is the way in which many people can read the same scriptures and each person will have a unique experience that rises up out of his or her own life context in that moment. When I read Scripture, I bring all of my memories and relationships, my feelings and dreams to the text. The prayer that rises out of *lectio divina* responds to my life experience. When I read the same scriptural passage again at another time in my life, my experience will be different.

THE FOUR MOVEMENTS OF *LECTIO DIVINA*

Lectio divina is a process of prayer that involves four steps or movements often summarized as reading, reflecting, responding, and resting. I will be looking more closely at each movement in later chapters, but I want to provide you with an overview here and general understanding of how the process unfolds. I have chosen words to describe each movement that I hope will help illuminate the dynamic of that particular step and especially open the practice to those outside of the Christian tradition.

LECTIO: SETTLING AND SHIMMERING

The traditional Latin name for this first movement is called *lectio*, which simply means "reading." To begin, settle into your prayer space, let go of distractions, and open yourself to an experience of prayer. In your initial encounter with the text, read the text through slowly and listen for a word or phrase that beckons you, addresses you, unnerves you, disturbs you, stirs you, or seems especially ripe with meaning—what I describe as a word or phrase that "shimmers." Gently repeat this word or phrase to yourself in the silence.

MEDITATIO: SAVORING AND STIRRING

The traditional Latin name for this second movement is *meditatio*, which means simply "reflection" or "thinking." The invitation in this movement is to read the whole text again, and then take some time to savor the word or phrase that shimmers by allowing it to unfold in your imagination. Listen for what images, feelings, and memories are stirring and welcome into your heart whatever comes.

ORATIO: SUMMONING AND SERVING

The traditional name for the third movement is *oratio*, which means "speech" or "address" and in this sense refers to verbal prayer. In this movement the particular dynamic is listening for how the things that have been stirring within you in response to the word or phrase connect to some aspect of your everyday life. Prayer arises spontaneously when you allow your heart to be touched by this entering of God into your experience and you are drawn to respond in prayer.

The assumption of *lectio* practice is that the text is multilayered and able to respond to us in each concrete and unique moment of our lives. After savoring the inner movements, we listen for an invitation from God in light of our current circumstances. This invitation may be a summons toward a new awareness or action. We are summoned to stretch ourselves beyond our usual limits. We ask for the grace to have our hearts changed by what we have heard and to live out that change in concrete ways. Ultimately, our response to this invitation is meant to move beyond our personal concerns, and be of service to others.

CONTEMPLATIO: SLOWING AND STILLING

The fourth movement, *contemplatio* in Latin, means "contemplation." This movement is about slowing yourself down and resting into the still presence of God. The idea is to simply *be*, rather than trying to *do* anything. This is a time for offering gratitude for God's presence in this time of prayer and stilling yourself in silence.

Invitation to Practice *Lectio Divina*

I invite you now to move into the practice of *lectio divina*. The following is meant as an introductory way of entering into the experience of prayer. (The chapters in Part Two will break open each individual movement in much more depth and detail.) This experience now is about entering into the rhythm of *lectio divina*; allowing yourself to sink into silence and spaciousness, begin to explore its contours. Try not to worry about whether you are getting it "right." The four movements are a process of contemplative unfolding, and there may be times when you end up praying "out of order" or with only one movement because that is how your heart is being led. As you begin your prayer, open yourself to trust in the way the Spirit is moving in you.

In future chapters I will make several suggestions for possible sacred texts, and you are welcome to follow these or choose other sacred texts. For this first attempt, I suggest this passage from Isaiah as your first text for prayer:

> For as the rain and the snow come down from
> heaven,
> and do not return there until they have watered the
> earth,
> making it bring forth and sprout,

giving seed to the sower and bread to the eater,
so shall my word be that goes out from my mouth;
it shall not return to me empty,
but it shall accomplish that which I purpose,
and succeed in the thing for which I sent it.

For you shall go out in joy,
and be led back in peace.

—Isaiah 55:10–12a

First Movement—*Lectio*: Settling and Shimmering

Find a comfortable position where you can remain alert and yet also relax your body. Bring your attention to your breath and allow a few moments to become centered. If you find yourself distracted at any time, gently return to the rhythm of your breath as an anchor for your awareness. Allow yourself to settle into this moment and become fully present.

Read the passage above from Isaiah once or twice through slowly and listen for a word or phrase that feels significant right now, that is capturing your attention even if you don't know why. Gently repeat this word to yourself in the silence.

Second Movement—*Meditatio*: Savoring and Stirring

Read the text again, and then allow the word or phrase that caught your attention in the first movement to spark your imagination. Savor the word or phrase with all of your senses; notice what smells, sounds, tastes, sights, and feelings are evoked. Then listen for what images, feelings, and memories are stirring, welcoming them in and then savoring and resting into this experience.

Third Movement—*Oratio*:
Summoning and Serving

Read the text a third time, and then listen for an invitation rising up from your experience of prayer so far. Considering the word or phrase and what it has evoked for you in memory, image, or feeling, what is the invitation? This invitation may be a summons toward a new awareness or action.

Fourth Movement—*Contemplatio*:
Slowing and Stilling

Move into a time for simply resting in God and allowing your heart to fill with gratitude for God's presence in this time of prayer. Slow your thoughts and reflections even further and sink into the experience of stillness. Rest in the presence of God and allow yourself to simply be. Rest here for several minutes. Return to your breath if you find yourself distracted.

Closing

Gently connect with your breath again and slowly bring your awareness back to the room, moving from inner experience to outer experience. Give yourself some time of transition between these moments of contemplative depth and your everyday life. Consider taking a few minutes to journal about what you experienced in your prayer.

Suggested Texts for *Lectio Divina*:
The Power of Words

Each chapter in this book will end with a selection of suggested texts for your *lectio divina* practice, with a different theme connected to the elements we are exploring in that chapter. Many of my suggestions will come from the Hebrew and Christian scriptures, and some chapters will also include texts from the Rule of Benedict and from other religious traditions as a way of showing the breadth of material to work with. It will also invite you into engagement with the wisdom of other faith traditions.

> Hear, O Israel: The LORD is our God, the LORD alone. You shall love the LORD your God with all your heart, and with all your soul, and with all your might. Keep these words that I am commanding you today in your heart. Recite them to your children and talk about them when you are at home and when you are away, when you lie down and when you rise. Bind them as a sign on your hand, fix them as an emblem on your forehead, and write them on the doorposts of your house and on your gates.
>
> —*Deuteronomy 6:4–9*

> Your words were found, and I ate them,
> and your words became to me a joy
> and the delight of my heart;
> for I am called by your name,
> O Lord, God of hosts.
>
> —*Jeremiah 15:16*

> Rejoice in the Lord, O you righteous.
> Praise befits the upright.
> Praise the Lord with the lyre;
> make melody to him with the harp of ten strings.
> Sing to him a new song;
> play skillfully on the strings, with loud shouts.
> For the word of the Lord is upright,
> and all his work is done in faithfulness.
> He loves righteousness and justice;

the earth is full of the steadfast love of the Lord.
By the word of the Lord the heavens were made,
and all their host by the breath of his mouth.

—*Psalm 33:1–6*

One ever-flowing pen inscribed the names
Of all the creatures, in their kinds and colors;
But which of us would seek to pen that record?
Or if we could, how great the scroll would be.

How can one describe Thy beauty and might of Thy
    Works?
And who has power to estimate Thy Bounty, O
    Lord?
All creation emerging from Thy One Word,
Flowing out like a multitude of rivers.

—*from Sikh Morning Prayer*[8]

No longer a stranger, you listen all day to these
    crazy love-words. Like a bee you fill hundreds of
    homes with honey, though yours is a long flight
    from here.

No mirror ever became iron again; No bread ever
    became wheat; No ripened grape ever became
    sour fruit. Mature yourself and be secure from a
    change for the worse. Become the light.

Only from the heart
Can you touch the sky.

—*Rumi*

For Reflection

What are the ideas you have about yourself that get in the way of prayer and your relationship with God?

What does it mean to you when you are asked to allow God's imagination to work through you?

What are the biggest challenges for you in "not-doing"? Of waiting? Of resting? Of being nonproductive?

What do you most desire from your prayer practice?

Have you ever heard the voice of God in your life experience? If so, what was that like?

Have you ever felt the call to service? If so, how did you respond?

CHAPTER TWO

AT THE HEART OF
LECTIO DIVINA

Benedictine Spirituality and Heart-Centered Prayer

*In the innermost depths of my heart I transcend the
bounds of my created personhood and discover
within myself the direct unmediated presence of the
living God. Entry into the deep heart means that I
experience myself as God-sourced, God-enfolded,
God-transfigured.*

—*Kallistos Ware*, Paths to the Heart:
Sufism and the Christian East

All that we know about the life of Benedict of Nursia and his
twin sister Scholastica comes from a collection called the
Dialogues, written by Pope Gregory I, which attribute several
miracles to him. The son of a Roman nobleman, Benedict began
his monastic vocation as a young man by living as a hermit for
three years in a cave at Subiaco. As his reputation for wisdom
grew, however, he was called back into service to the world when
a community of monks asked him to be their abbot. They eventually tried to poison him, and so he left the community to establish several monasteries of his own and began writing the
Benedictine rule.

This rule of life was strongly influenced by the writings of Christian theologian John Cassian and previous monastic rules. Because he was the first to articulate the principles of shared common life in such an accessible form, Benedict is considered to be the founder of Western monasticism. It is important to remember that his rule was composed for laypeople, not for priests, and served as a guide to both the practical and the spiritual needs of a community. Its foundation is *ora et labora*, work and prayer, a life held in balance between the two. Benedict believed that work, far from being the occupation of slaves and menials—the common belief of his time—was a way toward goodness. Thus, his communities were places of radical equality and mutuality, where both rich and poor worked alongside one another, gave up their possessions, and committed themselves to a life of discipline and prayer.

Today there is a renaissance of monastic spirituality and practice for laypeople living beyond the monastery walls. Oblates, who are people committed to living a Benedictine way of life in the world, are joining communities in large numbers. What drew me to becoming a Benedictine oblate was the profoundly balanced way of life that Benedict proposed in his rule. While written for people living within monasteries, the wisdom can be easily extended "beyond the walls." Benedict believed that everything was sacred—even kitchen utensils were to be treated as reverently as the vessels used on the altar. The routine of fixed hour prayer, with its reading of Scripture and saying of prayers regularly throughout the day and evening, becomes a way of sanctifying time. Benedictine spirituality calls me to move through my day mindfully, remembering the sacredness of each act, each object, each encounter with another person. In a world where busyness is praised and productivity is the sole measure of value, the monastic path offers me support and guidance in choosing to live in a contemplative way, with more presence in everything I do.

THE SIGNIFICANCE OF THE HEART IN SPIRITUALITY

Since I not only have a body but am some-body, this ingathering and outpouring finds expression in my pulsating heart. Located at the center of my body, at the intersection of its horizontal and its vertical axes, halfway between sex organs and brain, my heart constantly takes in and sends out the blood which keeps my body alive. As long as the heart is alive, it constantly sends forth and takes in.

—David Steindl-Rast

The heart is an ancient metaphor for the seat of our whole being. To be "whole-hearted" means to bring our entire selves before God—our intellect, our emotional life, our dreams and intuitions, and our deepest longings. The heart is both active and receptive. The heart listens, but also hears; the heart savors and supplies nourishment to be savored; the heart responds but is also open to the call of others.

The heart is also where we cultivate compassion for ourselves and for others; where we discover we are intertwined with other human beings, with all creatures, and with the Divine. In his essay "How Do We Enter the Heart?" Orthodox theologian and bishop Kallistos Ware describes the heart as "at one and the same time a physical reality—the bodily organ located in our chest—and also a psychic and spiritual symbol. Above all it signifies integration and relationship: the integration and unification of the total person within her or himself, and at the same time the centering and focusing of the total person upon God."[1]

Across religious traditions, the heart is the dwelling place for God. In Matthew 6:6, for example, Jesus advises, "But when you pray, go into your room, close the door and pray to your Father, who is unseen. Then your Father, who sees what is done in secret, will reward you." This passage is interpreted in Eastern Christian tradition as "go into the chambers of your heart." In his letter to the Romans 5:5, Paul writes, "God's love has been poured into our hearts through the Holy Spirit that has been given to us." In the Hebrew scriptures, the word for heart is *lev,* and it is not only the seat of the emotions but also the center of thought. In one sense the heart *is* the mind, encompassing all thoughts, including the emotions.

For Hindus, the Sanskrit word for heart, *hridaya*, also means the center of the world, while Muslims describe the heart as the throne of the All-Merciful. The basic term in Arabic for the heart is *qalb*, which means change and transformation. The heart is the *barzakh,* or isthmus, between this world and the next, between visible and invisible worlds, between the human realm and the realm of the Spirit.[2] In Islamic tradition, the heart affects how we perceive the world; when it is infected with anger or jealousy, the heart's vison is distorted, unable to see the world as it truly is.

WHAT IS HEART-CENTERED PRAYER?

Lectio divina is the practice of being present to each moment in a heart-centered way. When we pray *lectio* we see sacred text as God's living words being spoken to our hearts in the moment. The practice allows us to encounter God in an active and intimate way. The invitation of *lectio divina*, therefore, is to cultivate a heart-centered intimacy with the sacred texts that is a different way of engaging them than pure interpretive reasoning. *Lectio divina* asks us to listen, savor, and respond—not simply understand their meaning. The purpose of this practice is that we gradually bring these qualities of being to the whole of our lives and everything is potentially a sacred text through which God can speak to us.

Contemporary spirituality author Norvene Vest describes the Hebrew scriptures as speaking of the heart as "the locus of the active-receptive relationship with God in spiritual formation. For the early Hebrews, the heart was the organ of capacity for God's very self: It was the locus not only of choice and motive but also of one's fundamental orientation toward life. In the heart, we are formed and reformed into the person we most long to be." She goes on to say:

> *Lectio*'s structure is designed to form this essential center of our being, which is our capacity for God, our disposition to act, our heart/will. *Lectio* asks that we lay our life issues alongside the patterns described in scripture and find there a template that helps us be who we are fully meant to be.[3]

Concern for the heart means concern for the sacred center of our innermost being. The book of Proverbs advises us to take care of our hearts with utmost concern, which is the biblical expression for spiritual practice. In biblical theology, "heart" means the center, the source, the taproot of our being. We cannot even say that the bodily heart becomes here a symbol for a purely spiritual concept. "Heart" stands for an insight that is conceived before we ever begin to think conceptually. As Kallistos Ware writes,

> For biblical authors, the heart does not signify the feelings and emotions, for those are located lower down in the guts and entrails. The heart designates, on the contrary, the inwardness of our human personhood in its full spiritual depth.... The heart is in this way the place where we formulate our primary hope, where we express our sense of direction, our purpose in life. It is the moral center, the determinant of action, and so it corresponds in part to what we mean today by the conscience. It is the seat of the memory, understood not just as the recollection of things past but as deep self-awareness at the present moment.[4]

The infinite love of God has been poured out directly into our hearts. The Holy Spirit is often described as a dynamic power, active in the world. We might imagine the Spirit being poured into our hearts and coursing through our veins, flowing through us and meant to flow out into the world through service and love.

For some of you it might be challenging to set aside your desire to understand the interpretation and historical context of the scriptures before entering into prayer. *Lectio divina* is not meant to be a replacement for serious and scholarly study of scriptural texts. Certainly the historical and literary interpretations are an essential tool for claiming a healthy and balanced understanding of what the scriptures have to offer us. However, this is the realm of Scripture study, and what too often happens is that we allow such analysis to become our sole relationship to these stories.

Ultimately, the movement of *lectio divina* brings us to greater and greater compassion for ourselves and for others. Our circle of compassion widens as we engage in regular practice. The Latin root of the word for compassion literally means "suffering together with another." The Hebrew word *rechem* in the singular form means "womb," and it shares the same root with *racham*, which means to have compassion for others. Being compassionate means to enter into the deep wounded heart of the world and to birth a relationship of mutuality with the poor, the sick, the imprisoned, the homeless, the dying, the exploited, the oppressed, and all with whom God identifies.

Invitation to Practice: Heart-Centered Prayer

I invite you into a very simple heart-centered practice. It takes less than five minutes and can be done almost anywhere, but can completely shift your grounding and awareness so you respond to the world from a more heart-centered place. This is also a powerful way to enter into your *lectio divina* practice, as a time of preparation, grounding, and centering.

1. Begin by becoming aware of your body. Notice how your body is feeling, simply being present to sensations you are experiencing. Welcome in both the body's delight and the body's discomfort. If there are any areas of tension, see if you can soften into those places.

2. Shift your focus to your breath, deepening it gently. As you inhale, imagine God breathing life into you. As you exhale, allow yourself to experience a moment of release and surrender into this time and place, becoming fully aware. Take several cycles of breath and simply notice this life-sustaining rhythm that continues, moment by moment, even when you are unaware of it.

3. In your imagination, gently allow your breath to carry your awareness from your head—your thinking, analyzing, judging center—down to your heart, a place of greater integration, feeling, and intuition. This movement is not forced, but more of a permission. Imagine your heart as a great magnetic force drawing your energy into your center.

4. Place your hand on your chest, over your heart, to experience a physical connection with your heart center and help draw your awareness to this place. Rest in this heart-centered space for a while. Release expectations of what the experience will be, staying open to the surprising ways of God.

5. Imagine drawing your breath down into your heart center as you inhale. Begin to notice what you are feeling right now in this moment, without judging or trying to change it. Allow your breath to soften the space around your heart. Take a few moments

to be present to whatever it is you are feeling. Make room within yourself for this experience—whether grief, anger, boredom, joy, anxiety, serenity—without pushing it away. Welcome in the full spectrum of who you are.

6. Taking another breath, call to mind the spark of God that the ancient monks and mystics tell us dwells in our heart. Bring the infinite compassion of God that lives within you to whatever you are feeling right now. You are not trying to change anything, but just gently hold yourself in this space. As you experience yourself filling with compassion for your own experience, imagine breathing that compassion out into the world and connecting to other hearts—both human and animal—beating across the world in a rhythm of love. Allow that love to expand within you with each inhale. As you exhale, imagine allowing it to expand into the space around you, getting wider with each breath. Fill with gratitude for whatever your experience has been and for the gift of a holy pause in which to simply rest in what is.

7. Gently allow your breath to bring your awareness back to the room and take a moment to name what you noticed in this experience.

This practice is especially powerful when you find yourself feeling tender-hearted, anxious, sad, or any emotion that is uncomfortable or confusing. The idea is not to resolve the emotion or figure it out, but to simply allow it to have a moment of space within you. When you need to make a decision about something, try grounding yourself in this way first, connecting with your heart center to access the wisdom of compassion within you. I invite you to pause for this practice once or twice a day over the next few days and see what you notice.

Suggested Texts for *Lectio Divina*: Heart

A new heart I will give you, and a new spirit I will put within you; and I will remove from your body the heart of stone and give you a heart of flesh. I will put my spirit within you, and make you follow my statutes and be careful to observe my ordinances.

—Ezekiel 36:26–27a

Yet even now, says the Lord,
return to me with all your heart,
with fasting, with weeping, and with mourning;
rend your hearts and not your clothing,
Return to the Lord, your God,
for he is gracious and merciful,
slow to anger, and abounding in steadfast love,
and relents from punishing.

—Joel 2:12–13

Do not store up for yourselves treasures on earth, where moth and rust consume and where thieves break in and steal; but store up for yourselves treasures in heaven, where neither moth nor rust consumes and where thieves do not break in and steal. For where your treasure is, there your heart will be also.

—Matthew 6:19–21

The deliciousness of milk and honey is the reflection of the pure heart:
from that heart the sweetness of every sweet thing is derived.

The heart is the substance, and the world the
    accident:
how should the heart's shadow be the object of the
    heart's desire?
Is that pure heart the heart that is enamored of
    riches or power,
or is submissive to this black earth and water of the
    body,
or to vain fancies it worships in the darkness for the
    sake of fame?
The heart is nothing but the Sea of Light:
is the heart the place of vision of God—and then
    blind?
                            —*Rumi, III, 2265–9*

When the heart is hard and parched up,
come upon me with a shower of mercy.

When grace is lost from life,
come with a burst of song.

When tumultuous work raises its din on all sides
    shutting me out from beyond,
come to me, my lord of silence, with thy peace and
    rest.
When my beggarly heart sits crouched, shut up in a
    corner,
break open the door, my king, and come with the
    ceremony of a king.

When desire blinds the mind with delusion and
    dust, O thou holy one,
thou wakeful, come with thy light and thy thunder.[5]
                        —*Rabindranath Tagore*

For Reflection

At what times in your life have you made decisions from your intuitive, feeling heart rather than your rational, intellect head?

What emotions stir within you when you know you are acting from your heart?

What do you notice when you simply allow yourself to feel the way you do without judgment and you bring compassion to your experience?

Are there experiences in life that have hardened your heart?

THE ROLE OF
SPIRITUAL PRACTICE

Cultivating Ways of Being in the World

*I have come to know that spirituality is eminently a
practical science—it concerns what we do when we
get up in the morning, how we spend our day, how
we go to bed at night—and specifically how much
time and energy we are willing to dedicate to the
practice of prayer and meditation.*

—Cyprian Consiglio, Prayer in the
Cave of the Heart

In his book *Worship and Spirituality*, theologian Don Saliers
describes spirituality as "our embodied humanity fully alive
before God and neighbor, stretched by story, stretched by
touch, stretched by song, stretched by eating and drinking,
bathing, anointing."[1] This description of the spiritual life
points to its embodied character through particular practices.
In our daily patterns of loving, caring, and working, we are
following a spiritual path of sorts, whether we are conscious of
it or not. The shape of our lives reflects our priorities and ultimate values. We nurture intentional and conscious choices
about how to shape these patterns and ways of being through

commitment to regular spiritual practices of prayer. We can help shape the persons we are becoming by the practices we choose to commit ourselves to and live into as they transform us. Such practices are used to regulate and shape our lives, on the assumption that changing our habits can change our perceptions and ideas as well.

In their book on this topic, *Practicing Our Faith*, Dorothy Bass and Craig Dykstra describe Christian spiritual practices as shared patterns of activity in and through which life together takes shape over time in response to God. Woven together, our collective practices help form a way of life. When you participate in spiritual practice you are embodying a specific kind of wisdom about what it means to be human in relationship to God.

Spiritual practices also connect us more deeply to our faith traditions and faith communities. Practices are historically rooted and endure over long periods. Through practice we are called to shape our lives in intentional ways, drawing on ancient wisdom passed down through generations of story and tradition. Spiritual practice can help us think about and live the spiritual life beyond the individualism of the dominant culture in order to disclose the shared and communal quality of our lives. While they help us shape our lives in relation to God, they also help us connect to one another, across communities and through space and time.

When we practice contemplative ways of praying and living, we slow down, which allows us to really see and hear God at work. We savor our experiences rather than consume them; relationships become heightened. We become more present to each moment and discover the luminosity of everyday life. Daily tasks feel less burdensome as we remember everything is holy and we become aware of the gift hidden in each moment. We learn to cultivate the ability to be present to the tides of transition in life and respond from a more calm and centered place. We develop compassion for our own challenges and in turn we widen our compassion for others. These have been some of the fruits of a *lectio divina* practice for me.

But be warned—establishing and maintaining a spiritual practice is not easy. Spiritual practice will at times be challenging because as we slow down and move into silence we begin to hear our own inner voices that much more loudly. Our compulsions suddenly become more apparent. We encounter boredom and anxiety, restlessness, the desire to be someplace else. We want to turn on the radio or the television to fill the air with sound. We want to make a phone call, or write our list of things to accomplish for the day. We are offered a continual array of choices: Do I stay present to this moment or do I get up and do something else? In solitude we may find ourselves in a wrestling match with the demons of boredom and restlessness, which the ancient monks called *acedia*.

To ease the challenges of spiritual practice, three key spiritual virtues in Benedictine monastic life are stability, obedience, and conversion. Outside of the monastery, cultivating these virtues can help anyone create a supportive context for contemplative prayer and the rhythms of *lectio divina*.

Stability: Holding Fast to Your Prayer Practice

For monastic men and women, stability means making a commitment to a particular monastery for a lifetime. Through serene times and times of hardship, these religious are called to stay present and do the difficult work of being in relationship. For those of us living spiritual lives outside of the monastery walls, the quality of stability is somewhat different—it means making a commitment to be faithful to our life circumstances even at the most challenging times. Stability roots us in whatever place or situation we find ourselves in; we are committed to facing adversity, not run away at the first sign of difficulty. This might apply to a marriage or friendship, to our work life, or simply to the daily challenges with which we find ourselves confronted. For example, my own primary community is my marriage to my husband of sixteen years. Marriage is for me one of the hardest and most rewarding commitments of my life. In marriage or other deeply felt partnerships, there is a delicate dance of mutuality and attentiveness to the needs of another. It can be difficult because it means negotiating daily life and dreams with another person who has his or her own vision of the world. But the rewards of approaching such relationships with the quality of stability include finding a place where we feel cherished and profoundly loved.

In the same way, we bring the quality of stability to our *lectio divina* practice because it reminds us to keep showing up even when things become difficult or challenging. When we begin a new practice or renew our commitment to one, at first we may have no problem making time for our prayer each day. But then as time goes on, we find our attention wandering or life events interfering. With the commitment to stability, we remember that the practice is to continue being present, beginning again and again.

The sounds of Scripture, once so comforting, now seem dry and unstimulating. We may have days when the tyranny of our inner voices and thoughts is alive within us, or we begin to connect with deep wells of grief that come from having rejected our most authentic selves time after time. Stability is about the ways we stay committed to our prayer practice through these challenges. This is the heart of practice. It is easy to pray when it feels easy, but the spiritual life isn't about always seeking what feels best.

That is why practicing *lectio divina* involves a great deal of patient waiting and attending:

> It is possible to become obsessed with technique and lose
> sight of the working of grace, of God's initiative. Prayer is
> not "magic" … we do not conjure up God, we do not bring

God down from heaven, and we do not make ourselves holy. We dispose ourselves, we stop, we listen, we wait, we watch, we make ourselves available, and we put ourselves in situations and environments that are conducive to prayer and meditation. And then we wait for the working of grace, like the bride awaiting the bridegroom.[2]

Many of us come to prayer with great hopes and expectations. We want to experience inner peace, clarity, wisdom, guidance—often right away—and we think the fruits will come to us just by simply showing up for practice. But in reality, there are many days when nothing seems to happen. We are not moved by a word or phrase, or our inner response feels dry or desolate. The invitation arising may feel trite or inconsequential. There may be many occasions when God doesn't seem to be "saying" anything (or at least not what we wanted to hear).

Often our frustration arises from a subconscious "task-oriented" approach to *lectio,* where it is only "successful" if we receive something of measurable value from the experience. It is a natural extension of the way many of us live our lives, valuing only what seems productive to us at the time. This is where we return again to the quality of stability. We are invited to make a commitment to the process through the challenges and joys as well as the periods where prayer is dull or doesn't inspire.

Hospitality plays a role here as well, which we will explore further in Chapter Six. Can we welcome in those moments of prayer—and by extension those moments in our lives—when boredom may set in? Can we attune ourselves to the even more subtle movements of grace? Can we simply rest in the presence of the Holy One without expectation of some result we can see? Can we welcome all the parts of ourselves and our experience into our prayer?

Sometimes we think we need to travel on an exotic adventure to discover something of God's radical call to us. Or we try a variety of practices, each one not feeling completely satisfying, in part because we never allow ourselves to enter into its full depth and invitation. We may move on when we get bored or don't achieve instant peace or enlightenment. Writer Esther de Waal describes stability this way:

> You will find stability at the moment you discover that God is everywhere, that you do not need to seek Him elsewhere, that He is here, and if you do not find Him here it is useless to go and search for Him elsewhere because it is not Him that is absent from us, it is we who are absent from Him…. It is important to recognize that it is useless to seek God somewhere else. If you cannot find Him here you will not find Him anywhere else.[3]

OBEDIENCE: LISTENING FOR GOD

The root of the word *obedience* means "to hear," and this practice is about making a commitment to listen for God's voice in the world and respond when you hear God's invitation to you. Obedience is a difficult concept for modern Western thinkers, but consider it as a way of deep listening for the Holy in all dimensions of your life. The second essential aspect of this listening is a response—are you willing not only to make the time and space to listen for God's call but also to respond with your full self? The paradoxical outcome of obedience is an *inner freedom*, because we slowly learn to distinguish God's voice from the many other voices that demand our attention.

As I will explore in Chapter Seven, the third movement of *lectio divina* focuses on listening for the invitation that arises from our prayer to a new awareness or action. When we cultivate the quality of obedience in our lives, we bring this commitment to listen deeply for the invitation being whispered from the depths of our heart, and we are ready to respond, to open ourselves to changing our lives if that is what is asked of us.

Sometimes obedience also means praying as we are led, rather than praying as we set out to. The four movements of *lectio divina* can be helpful to move through in a linear way when we are learning the practice. However, sometimes our prayer, especially prayer of the heart, emerges in more of a spiral. Different aspects of the prayer call us for attention at different moments.

Since *lectio divina* wasn't codified into its four stages until the Middle Ages, we might do better in our own time to consider these four movements as a spiral or web, each interconnected with the other. Reading in this way is not a linear act. This is in part why we enter the space of the heart, which is the integrative place within us and can experience nonlinear ways of being. As Maria Lichtmann describes in *The Teacher's Way: Teaching and the Contemplative Life*,

> Each stage is present to and within all the others like the interdependent parts of a mandala or a circle dance. If we see each aspect of *lectio divina* at the corners of a mandala, they can all point us to the center, the sacred. We can invert Guigo's ladder metaphor to one of descent or deepening, or we can bend it to form a never-ending circle. The journey of contemplation is not so much a straightforward journey, charted in stages of "progress," but a spiraling round the center of one's own being and life. In the view of a contemporary Carthusian, the ladder of *lectio divina* is a "journey towards the heart." … Guigo's "ladder," then, is an *intuitive* one, the destiny of which is the heart's intimacy and openness to and with all.[4]

When I approach a sacred text in this way, I am entrusting myself to its words, opening my heart to be shaped and transformed. I come with a willingness to be obedient to what it demands of me, meaning that *lectio divina* is about hearing and responding, knowing that when we begin our prayer we don't know how we will be called.

A participant in one of my *lectio divina* workshops describes her experience this way:

> For they are life to those who find them,
> and healing to all their flesh.
>
> —*Proverbs 4:22*

> As I ponder on these words from Proverbs I am upheld by the vast ocean of grace which has been my swimming place for most of my life. Over and over again the words of Scripture, of the poet, of the lyricist, of the writer of fiction and memoir have been a healing force for my emotional and physical body.
>
> Silent contemplation of the words that cross my path have been a constant blessing. Healing from two bouts of breast cancer, from the ups and downs of a marriage now in its forty-ninth year, from the shocks and surprises of forcing myself to live on my "growing edge"—all have been nurtured by the power of words kept close to my heart. (*Barbara Miller*)

Obedience means allowing the sacred texts of our lives to support us through life and honoring the wisdom they bring us for the challenges we face.

CONVERSION: ALWAYS OPEN TO CHANGE

Conversion for me essentially means making a commitment to always be surprised by God. Conversion is the counterpart to stability. If stability calls us to be rooted and persistent, conversion is the recognition that we are all on a journey and always changing. God is always offering us something new within us. Conversion is a commitment to total inner transformation and a free response both to the ways God is calling us and to new images of

God. Contemporary scholar and poet Eugene Peterson describes it this way:

> What we must never be encouraged to do, although all of us are guilty of it over and over, is to force Scripture to fit our experience. Our experience is too small; it's like trying to put the ocean into a thimble. What we want is to fit into the world revealed by Scripture, to swim in its vast ocean.[5]

Several years ago I was going through a period of intense discernment. I had finished graduate school and found that my desires were no longer in alignment with the path I had initially imagined for myself. I spent long periods of time in silence and solitude, engaging all of the essential techniques for discernment I had learned in my studies and previous practice, taking this very seriously because this was my life path I was pondering. Then one night I had a dream about koala bears trying to get a map out of my hands so they could play with me. In my reflection time that followed, I discovered a playful God who was calling me to take myself and my discernment far less seriously than I had been. I love to laugh, but in my longing to discover the next path, I had forgotten how playfulness is woven into the heart of the universe. Trappist monk and progressive religious thinker Thomas Merton has a marvelous quotation about this at the end of his book *New Seeds of Contemplation*:

> What is serious to men is often very trivial in the sight of God. What in God might appear to us as "play" is perhaps what He Himself takes most seriously. At any rate the Lord plays and diverts Himself in the garden of His creation, and if we could let go of our own obsession with what we think is the meaning of it all, we might be able to hear His call and follow Him in His mysterious, cosmic dance.[6]

We bring a commitment to conversion to our *lectio* practice by remembering that there are always more opportunities for growth, that the sacred texts offer us an endless depth of wisdom that we can never exhaust. We come to our prayer setting aside expectations and enter into a willingness to be surprised by God; even if we have read the scriptures many times before, we open our hearts to transformation again and again. And if we are tempted to take our *lectio* practice too seriously, we are reminded of God's playful nature and the one who dances creation into being. Conversion calls us to release our hold on our certainty and move more into an openhearted place of unknowing and accepting the great mystery that pulses at the heart of everything.

Spirituality and prayer are about a journey toward greater freedom and the capacity to love. As we commit to these practices of contemplative prayer, our understanding of God becomes more expansive, we discover ourselves in the arms of the Beloved, and as we grow in our experience of God's love for us, we also grow in our ability to love others—especially those who we dislike or who have been invisible to us. Benedictine scholar Michael Casey describes our encounter with God in the text as one that drags us

> beyond our own comfort zone into new territory and new adventures, it is an act by which we are drawn or even compelled to leave behind the boundaries that our self-hood has imposed upon our lives. We are called to transcend our own limited vision of the good life and accept something of the all-inclusiveness of God's plan for human fulfillment. The greatest enemy to this is our own willful refusal to budge beyond the closed circuit of our settled prejudices and pious routines.[7]

Lectio divina demands that we stay the course, that we listen with a willing heart, and that we open ourselves to ongoing radical transformation. Soul work is always challenging and calls us beyond our comfort zone. Prayer isn't about baptizing the status quo, but entering into dynamic relationship with the God who always makes things new. Scripture challenges our ingrained patterns of belief, our habitual attitudes and behavior. Conversion is about maintaining what the Buddhists call "beginner's mind," a reminder that we are called to approach our practice with the heart of a beginner. St. Benedict speaks to this practice when he describes his rule as a "little Rule for beginners" and calls us to "always begin again."

LECTIO DIVINA AS A PATH TO WISDOM

I invite you to reflect on how these three invitations—to obedience, stability, and conversion—might take root in your own life as you make a commitment to practicing contemplative ways of praying. As you practice *lectio divina* this week, consider how you are being invited to listen more deeply and respond. Contemplate the ways you want to move away from what is uncomfortable and unknown. Explore the ways you are invited to growth in each moment.

Ultimately, *lectio divina* is a path to wisdom. There is a rich wisdom tradition woven through the Hebrew and Christian scriptures and the literature of the mystics. Wisdom emerges from our experience; it is not learned through knowledge but through the heart. We gain wisdom from the moments of life that challenge us and stretch us. Wisdom is about the way we live our ordinary holy lives.

Some biblical scholars describe the wisdom tradition as "horizontal" rather than vertical revelation because it emerges from observations of daily life. This listening is accompanied by a readiness to respond. The method of wisdom literature is to stimulate our own reflection rather than provide us with answers. Wisdom means we are given responsibility for making choices and often have to act without complete certainty.

Stability, obedience, and conversion all call us to a path of wisdom, which is about growing in spiritual maturity. The practice of *lectio divina* invites us to a spirituality that takes seriously our daily lives and the living revelation of sacred texts.

Invitation to Practice: Commitment

Like all spiritual practices, *lectio divina* requires commitment—ideally, daily commitment—to achieve its full benefits. To help this, it is important to establish a regular time and space to practice.

Claim a Space

Is there a place in your home where you can engage in regular practice? All you need is a comfortable chair and perhaps a place to keep a candle, a journal, and a pen. You may already have a designated spot where you like to pray, and will continue to settle in there each day.

As we begin this journey, consider blessing your prayer space. Ask that it be a safe container for your prayer experience and that it hold you as you deepen your practice.

Establish a Time

Michael Casey writes that the word most often connected in monastic tradition with the practice of *lectio divina* is *assiduitas*, or assiduity, which connotes "constancy, continuity, perseverance." He describes four aspects to assiduity: making time, regularity, repetition, and perseverance. Making time for regular practice is the heart of how the scriptures shape us and our way of being in the world over time.

So the next step is to sit down with your calendar and write in a regular time for your practice. I suggest twenty to forty minutes each day and a longer session each week of about an hour to include reflection on what has been stirring in you over the last several days. It is very valuable to record your experiences in a journal or notebook, so you can look for patterns in your prayer that may reveal something new. While it may seem challenging to find enough minutes in the day, my experience is that my time spent in contemplative prayer renews me and focuses me in ways that help the rest of the day unfold with more ease and centeredness. I spend much less time feeling scattered or anxious about things because I have an inner point to which I can return again and again.

Be gentle with yourself, however. There will be days you miss your practice, so remember that St. Benedict writes in his rule, "Always we begin again." I love these four words and repeat them to myself often. We are called to recommit ourselves again and again. Each time we drift away, we are invited to return with our whole hearts. Sometimes we spend so much energy in criticizing ourselves for not achieving something perfectly that we never return to it. Release these judgments and simply return, knowing that the Sacred Presence dwelling within you welcomes you back each time.

Create an Opening Ritual and Gesture

Begin your practice by creating a ritual for your *lectio divina* experience that you will repeat each time you enter prayer. Turn off the phone, step away from your e-mail, lock the door, or ask not to be interrupted for this period of time. Have your journal and pen nearby, light a candle, and settle into the space. Find a comfortable position where you can remain alert and yet also soften your body: sitting upright in a chair works well. You might ring a chime as a way of helping you cross this threshold into a different kind of space. Incorporating gentle movement and gestures is another way to honor the body's participation in prayer and as a vessel of wisdom.

Here is a suggestion for moving into prayer with simple arm gestures. You can do this seated or standing:

1. Begin by leaning forward and touching the earth to reverence it as the source and matrix for your life.
2. Reach your arms overhead to welcome in the gifts of infinite wisdom from God, the Creator of all.
3. Reach your arms out wide to the sides to receive and connect to wisdom across space, in the human community, and remember that you join your prayers with a multitude of others.
4. Reach your arms back behind you to honor the generations who have prayed before you and who leave a great well of contemplative wisdom from which we can drink.
5. Touch your forehead, lips, and chest, over your heart, and ask that the sacred word of God be always on your mind, always in your speech, and always in your heart.
6. Bring your hands to prayer position in front of the heart to connect to the great wisdom dwelling within you.

Write a Blessing

As you begin your *lectio divina* practice, consider writing a blessing for beginning each time of prayer. A blessing is a call to the Spirit to sustain you in this loving and holy encounter with the One who is beyond all names. You might include qualities you hope to cultivate and a prayer to be able to listen fully to what is spoken in your heart. St. Benedict counsels us to begin any good work with prayer for guidance and the ability to respond.

I offer you my own here, but I suggest that you eventually write your own:

> As you step across the threshold into this new
>   beginning
> may your heart soften and make room for the blos-
>   soming
> of the Holy in new ways within.
>
> May you receive the words of the sacred texts
> as a love letter from the One who knit you in your
>   mother's womb.
>
> May you discover that the voice of the Holy One is
>   already calling,
> you need only sink into the silence and respond.

Call to mind and heart the community across the world that regards texts as sacred revelation from a source of wisdom far greater than our own. Join in prayer together with others unknown to you who sit in silence this very moment in a variety of meditation practices, seeking greater presence and compassion. Pray for those who can't find silence in their worlds or hearts. The following are two examples of simple blessings for beginning lectio divina written by participants in my workshops:

> Seduce me, O sacred word;
> enter my fertile heart
> and birth holiness within me. (Sally Brower)
>
> Beloved, may your words settle into the rhythm of
> my heartbeat and the rhythm of my breath until my
> whole being becomes attuned with your song of
> love. (Cheryl Macpherson)

Suggested Texts for *Lectio Divina*: Wisdom

Because *lectio divina* is a practice that cultivates wisdom, it can be fruitful to pray with some of the texts that describe wisdom's qualities and attributes in Scripture. Here are some suggested texts from the Hebrew scriptures:

Wisdom cries out in the street;
in the squares she raises her voice.
At the busiest corner she cries out;
at the entrance of the city gates she speaks:
"How long, O simple ones, will you love being simple?
How long will scoffers delight in their scoffing
and fools hate knowledge?
Give heed to my reproof;
I will pour out my thoughts to you;
I will make my words known to you."
—*Proverbs 1:20–23*

Happy are those who find wisdom,
and those who get understanding,
for her income is better than silver,
and her revenue better than gold.
She is more precious than jewels,
and nothing you desire can compare with her.
Long life is in her right hand;
in her left hand are riches and honour.
Her ways are ways of pleasantness,
and all her paths are peace.
She is a tree of life to those who lay hold of her;
those who hold her fast are called happy.
—*Proverbs 3:13–19*

For wisdom is more mobile than any motion;
because of her pureness she pervades and
    penetrates all things.
For she is a breath of the power of God,
and a pure emanation of the glory of the Almighty;
therefore nothing defiled gains entrance into her.
For she is a reflection of eternal light,
a spotless mirror of the working of God,
and an image of his goodness.
                    —*Wisdom of Solomon 7:24–26*

The Diamond Sutra was given its name by the
Buddha because of its ability to cut through illusion and "bring us to the shore of awakening."
    So you should view all of the fleeting world:
    A star at dawn, a bubble in the stream; a flash
    of lightning in a summer cloud; a flickering *lamp*,
    a phantom, and a dream.
                    —*Diamond Sutra, Section 32*[8]

For Reflection

What have been your most enduring commitments
in your life and what has helped you stick with these
commitments? What have been the biggest challenges in maintaining those commitments?

Have you ever felt called to action in ways other than
you originally planned? What was the source of the call?

When in your life have you felt "surprised by God"?

How would you define wisdom?

Who are the wise elders of your life?

"GIVE ME A WORD"

Choosing Texts for *Lectio Divina*

A sentence of words is a marvelous thing. Words
reveal. We are presented with reality, with truth that
makes our world larger, our relations richer. Words
get us out of ourselves and into a responsive relation-
ship with a larger world of time and space, things
and people.

—*Eugene Peterson*, Eat This Book:
A Conversation in the Art of Spiritual Reading

What is a sacred text? Traditionally it comes from a collection of
authorized religious writings, such as the Hebrew and Christian
scriptures. The desert mothers and fathers believed that God
spoke to them directly and intimately through the words of the
Bible, which was considered to be a privileged place to encounter
God. They would have memorized large passages of text because
books were rare and expensive; in the fourth century, for example, St. Pachomius stressed the need for all his monks to memorize the Psalter and the New Testament. It was out of this
tradition, furthermore, that St. Benedict wrote his rule. In it he
prescribes *lectio divina* as a central activity of the monk's day—
about three hours daily, with more on Sundays and during liturgical seasons like Lent. He also counsels that the source of

reading should come from Scripture or readings from one of the early church fathers, such as John Cassian:

> For anyone hastening on to the perfection of the monastic life, there are the teachings of the holy Fathers, the observance of which will lead him to the very heights of perfection. What page, what passage of the inspired books of the Old and New Testaments is not the truest of guides for human life? Or what book of the holy catholic Fathers does not resoundingly summon us along the true way to reach the Creator? Then, besides the Conferences of the Fathers, their Institutes and their Lives, there is also the rule of our holy father Basil. For observant and obedient monks, all these are nothing less than tools for the cultivation of virtues.[1]

EXPANDING OUR IDEA OF THE SACRED

The Hebrew and Christian scriptures and the writings of the early church fathers have remained the primary texts for *lectio divina* through most of the history of the Christian church. If we push the boundaries even further, we can consider that there are an enormous number of texts available to us today that would fall under the heading of "classic." That is because a classic is something—a work of art, a text, a story, a tradition, a symbol, an experience that lives on in memory—that has a surplus of meaning; it is a bearer of truth across time and space and cannot be definitively interpreted. In *The Analogical Imagination* theologian David Tracy develops the concept of the "classic" to help explain how religious truth and meaning are made manifest across time. For example, he describes the Exodus story as a classic event because it continues to be reinterpreted in new ways without losing its original spiritual power. This story has spoken across time to African slaves and later, in the American civil rights movement, as a way to inspire the march toward freedom. A classic is an avenue to understanding truth; it provokes us and confronts us in the present with the feeling that something else might be the case. Genuine classics transform our horizons. Great literature and art make manifest and reveal "ultimate reality"—namely, God's presence.

Using this wider definition of a classic, the pool of texts can disclose truth and expand our horizons to include the canon of religious texts from multiple religious traditions such as the Bhagavad Gita, the Buddhist and Yoga Sutras, and the Qur'an. Since the definition of a classic also includes art, music, events, and symbols, we can include these less traditional "texts" within the range of possibilities for our prayer.

The word *sacred* comes from the Latin *sacer,* meaning "restricted" or "set off." The term *sacer* is closely related to *numen,* meaning a mysterious power or god that is present in places and things, from which we have the word *numinous.* Various traditions around the world also have a term that correlates with *sacer.* In Hebrew the term is *qadosh*, in Greek *hagios*, and in Arabic *muqaddas.* The concept of the sacred is ancient. According to Greek mythology and most ancient cultures and religions, there was a radical distinction between what belongs to the realm of the sacred and what is considered profane. In his book *The Sacred and the Profane*, Mircea Eliade explains that the sacred always manifests itself as a reality different from normal realities. We become aware of the sacred when it shows itself as something different from the profane.

In *The Idea of the Holy*, Rudolf Otto describes the experience of the numinous as "the deepest and most fundamental element in all strong and sincerely felt religious emotion." It may come peacefully, "like a gentle tide, pervading the mind with a tranquil mood of deepest worship," or with more vigor "thrillingly vibrant and resonant, until at last it dies away and the soul resumes its 'profane', non-religious mood of everyday experience."[2] Such an encounter with the sacred can stir strong emotions in us.

Monastic spirituality at its core cultivates an ability to see more and more of the world as within the realm of the sacred, as worthy of our reverence and care. As previously mentioned, Benedict urged his monks to treat the kitchen utensils with the same reverence as the vessels of the altar. With these words Benedict gives us the foundation for expanding the kinds of texts we might choose for a *lectio divina* practice.

With the contemporary reclaiming of the practice of *lectio divina* for laypeople, there is in many circles concurrent support for expanding our notion of which texts are sacred and worthy of our engagement through prayer. From my perspective, sacred texts can include written texts within the canon of different religious traditions as well as texts that are not scripturally based, such as poetry and other kinds of prose. Even less traditional, we can expand our idea of what constitutes a sacred "text" by including those that fall under Tracy's definition of a classic and pray with art, music, poetry, nature, and our own life experience. For example, I love poetry and it is often my own daily nourishment for prayer. There are lines from poems that continue to sing to me across time and space, such as these words from David Whyte's marvelous poem *What to Remember When Waking*: "What you can plan is too small for you to live." I go back to this phrase again and again, continually discovering new layers for myself. It offers me a sacred invitation to release my own agenda in life and prayer. In the opening quotation to this chapter, Eugene Peterson describes words as revealing and enlarging our sense of the world. I love what his words evoke in me, but I would apply this idea equally to an expanded definition of sacred texts.

CHOOSING TEXTS FOR PRAYER

Throughout this book I offer suggested texts for prayer and meditation at the end of each chapter. In your own ongoing practice, however, there are a couple of approaches you can take for choosing your own texts.

LENGTH

In *lectio divina*, it is often better to select a brief passage for prayer, so feel free to divide a particular reading into smaller sections. For example, the longer gospel reading or psalm you have chosen could be used for two or three days, taking short excerpts from it. In general, a reading should be between two and seven lines long, but even one powerful line can lead to a fruitful prayer experience.

LECTIONARY READINGS

A lectionary is a collection of Hebrew and Christian scriptures that are assigned for worship on any given day or occasion. If you are part of a liturgical tradition—including Roman Catholic, Lutheran, and Episcopal churches—consider selecting a reading from the lectionary cycle. These readings are available both for Sundays and for each day of the week.[3] You could begin the Monday before and each day until Sunday choose a selection from one of the three readings. These offer a ripe place for prayerful reflection and enter us into texts which are being prayed by a wider community.

LECTIO CONTINUA

One of the ways the ancient monks prayed *lectio* was to select a book of the Bible and begin at the beginning, pray with the words until a particular word or phrase stopped them, and then pause there to allow their *lectio divina* to unfold. The next time they returned to the text, they picked up at the same place and continued forward from there, and so a particular book might sustain their prayer for many weeks. Casey recommends this as a practice for those who intend to commit to *lectio* over time because it means that we will pray with texts we otherwise might not linger over. You may want to avoid texts that challenge you or don't seem to offer you any nourishment on the surface, but prayer often means wrestling with ideas that are difficult for you. So I recommend this practice as another way to be in a sustained relationship to the text. In many ways, this is a practice of stability, of sustaining a relationship over time even when things get uncomfortable. To choose a book to pray with, you might consider consulting a spiritual director or someone who knows your faith journey well.

BEYOND THE BIBLE

St. Benedict also recommended noncanonical texts for prayer, such as the *Conferences* and *Institutes* of John Cassian; the stories of the desert fathers and mothers were also considered sources of profound wisdom. To find more of these, I recommend *Becoming Fire: Through the Year with the Desert Fathers and Mothers*—a compelling collection of brief stories and sayings of these *ammas* and *abbas* that lend themselves beautifully to daily prayer and *lectio divina*. Or you might consider praying with the sacred texts of other traditions in this way, noticing how the Holy One whispers to you across the boundaries of time and culture. There are many book series published these days that offer daily readings not only from saints such as Teresa of Avila and Augustine of Hippo, but also from poets like Rumi and Rainer Maria Rilke. All offer rich food for prayer.

If you would like to explore religious texts beyond the Christian canon, you might choose something from the holy books of other religious traditions. A good source is Bede Griffiths' collection of different scriptures in *Universal Wisdom: A Journey through the Sacred Wisdom of the World* or *One Heart: Universal Wisdom from the World's Scriptures* by Bonnie Louise Kuchler. Both of these books are organized thematically. And if you would like to explore texts beyond those of religious traditions, consider sacred poetry. Translator Stephen Mitchell has gathered a collection of sacred poetry from around the world in *The Enlightened Heart: An Anthology of Sacred Poetry*, and poet Jane Hirshfield offers an anthology of texts by women in *Women in Praise of the Sacred: 43 Centuries of Spiritual Poetry by Women*.

Another simple way to choose a text is to be alert in your own general reading, whether a novel or a magazine. When you come across a line that makes you want to pause or underline it, consider saving it for some *lectio divina* later on. You might include the sentence before and after to give it context, but this is a good way to honor the words that rise up to us in everyday life. I believe the scriptures can be a privileged place to experience the sustained wisdom of a community gathered over centuries, but other texts can serve equally well as vehicles for listening for grace and interior movement. In Part Three of this book I will break open more possibilities for praying with art, music, nature, and life experience as a sacred text.

I consider the word of God to be spoken through each moment; we become the vehicles for its expression, and so the Bible is one way to listen. Praying *lectio* cultivates in us a rhythm of moving more deeply into a presence to our everyday life so that we begin to see the Sacred pulsing in more and more places. Consider receiving the world as sacred text where God's word can speak. Notice in your own life whether there are poems, icons or other art, pieces of music, or places in nature that prompt in you a longing to spend time and savor the sacred voice whispering there. This is a form of practicing obedience—listening to where God wants to speak to you. Your daily prayer helps support this vision, which is a fruit of sustained practice.

OTHER FACTORS IN SELECTING TEXTS

REPETITION IN PRAYER

Repetition in prayer can be very valuable. I encourage you during your practice to return to a text you have prayed before that has been especially meaningful to you, that gave you a sense there was more waiting for you or a charge of unexpected energy from some unknown source. Rather than a "been there, done that" mentality, *lectio divina* cultivates in us a sense that each moment contains a vast and sacred depth. Each time we return to it we can unearth more treasure. "Repetition is the soul of genuine *lectio*," Michael Casey writes. "It is a right brain activity; we do not grasp the entire content immediately but in a circular manner. We read and advance, then we go back and read again. With each repetition, something new may strike us."[4]

The sacred scriptures offer wisdom across time and space, meeting us in each moment of our lives. If we are committed to conversion, then we recognize our own newness in each moment. Every day we are different persons from the day before, and so we can pray with the same text again and again and continue to receive its gifts. The repetition might be with the same scriptural passage, or with one of the images or memories stirred in the reflection movement of your prayer, or perhaps the invitation you heard felt like the beginning of something much richer and you want to allow time for this to unfold further.

AWARENESS OF THEMES

A common way to select a passage with which to pray is thematically. If I am struggling with busyness in my life and longing for more silence, I might turn to a passage such as "Be still and know that I am God" (Psalm 46:10) with which to pray. Or perhaps I am wrestling with a sense of dryness in my prayer and so I seek out passages that refer to experiences in the desert, such as the Israelites escaping from Egypt in the book of Exodus or Jesus' own temptations during his forty days in the desert.

When I lead retreats, classes, and prayer experiences I often choose a *lectio divina* passage in this way. For example, if I lead a retreat for the season of spring, I might offer this passage as a focus for participants:

> For now the winter is past,
> the rain is over and gone.
> The flowers appear on the earth;
> the time of singing has come,
> and the voice of the turtle-dove
> is heard in our land.

The fig tree puts forth its figs,
and the vines are in blossom;
they give forth fragrance.
Arise, my love, my fair one,
and come away.

—*Song of Songs 2:11–13*

In general, however, I counsel against using the thematic approach as a regular way of choosing texts for individual prayer. It can result in your approaching the scriptures as a sort of antidote for whatever you are experiencing, and so passages get taken out of context. Following either the lectionary cycle or the practice of *lectio continua* as outlined above can both invite you to encounter passages you wouldn't necessarily choose for yourself and help prevent you from sticking with only what is easy or comfortable. Otherwise, you may never be challenged by your practice of *lectio*, which is one of the benefits of praying with texts in a liturgical cycle of readings. It is especially effective when making a commitment to praying *lectio divina* regularly and consistently. We also enter into a community of prayer because we are joining with people praying these same texts around the world. Our solitary prayer becomes an act of communion in this way. With *lectio continua*, you can pray with any longer text from Scripture, or else from a prose work or a book of poems. When you come across a passage that feels especially alive with meaning, more than you have accessed in one session, feel free to return to it again and again.

There are also texts from Scripture that were written for a very specific intent and purpose, and thus don't lend themselves to praying *lectio divina*. The legal codes found in the books of Exodus and Leviticus in the Hebrew Bible are a good example of this, as are the genealogies of Genesis. It is also a good idea to ask a wise elder or spiritual director for recommendations of texts with which to pray. A spiritual director knows you and your journey well, and so would have more of a sense of where your growth places are. This is why the spiritual journey is a communal one, so you don't fall into the trap of becoming your own guide. Asking for the wisdom of another will be a rich contribution to your journey. You might have a soul friend, someone with whom you share your intimate longings and dreams, who could also give you good counsel.

Invitation to Practice: Varying Translations

If you have selected a passage from Scripture, consider looking up different translations of the text. The language of different editions and translations can vary quite a bit from one version to another. Looking at different translations can help you discover nuances of the text and see whether one resonates with you more than another. These examples of varying translations of Psalm 62:6–9 will give you a sense of how they can evoke different responses:

My soul, be at rest in God alone, from whom comes
   my hope.
God alone is my rock and my salvation, my secure
   height; I shall not fall.
My safety and glory are with God, my strong rock
   and refuge.
Trust God at all times, my people! Pour out your
   hearts to God our refuge! *Selah*
Mortals are a mere breath, the powerful but an
   illusion;
On a balance they rise; together they are lighter
   than air. (New American Bible)

He alone is my rock and my salvation,
my fortress; I shall not be shaken.
On God rests my deliverance and my honour;

my mighty rock, my refuge is in God.
Trust in him at all times, O people;
pour out your heart before him;
God is a refuge for us. *Selah* (New Revised
    Standard Version)

For You alone my soul waits in silence;
my hope is from the Beloved.

Enfolding me with strength and steadfast love,
my faith shall remain firm.

In the Silence rests my freedom and my guidance;
You are the heart of my heart,
my refuge is in the Silence.

Trust in Love at all times, O people;
pour out your heart to the Beloved;

Let Silence be a refuge for you. (Nan C. Merrill,
    Psalms for Praying)

God, the one and only—
    I'll wait as long as he says.
Everything I hope for comes from him,
    so why not?
He's solid rock under my feet,
    breathing room for my soul,
An impregnable castle:
    I'm set for life.
My help and glory are in God
    —granite-strength and safe-harbor-God—
So trust him absolutely, people,
    lay your lives on the line for him,
God is a safe place to be. (Eugene Peterson, *The
    Message*)

There are many editions and translations of the world's sacred texts, and in the resource section you will find a few choices to show the variety and perspectives that exist. And if you are familiar with another language, consider purchasing a Bible translated into that language. Sometimes when we see something on new terms, it can spark a different understanding.

Invitation to Practice: Learn by Heart

The desert monks memorized Scripture as a way to pray without ceasing. By committing a passage to memory, we bring it into our being, integrating the words more deeply into our lives. This is the true meaning of learning "by heart."

Once you have selected a passage for prayer, take some time to memorize the text prior to entering into the practice of *lectio divina*. Repeat the passage gently to yourself throughout the day—while riding the subway, driving, gardening, or doing dishes. You might write it down on a sticky note and carry it with you, or post it next to your computer so you can be reminded of it. Take the passage out for a walk with you and recite the words with the rhythm of your steps or your breathing as a way to connect the text with your body's experience.

Suggested Texts for *Lectio Divina*: Encountering the Sacred

Moses was keeping the flock of his father-in-law Jethro, the priest of Midian; he led his flock beyond the wilderness, and came to Horeb, the mountain of God. There the angel of the LORD appeared to him in a flame of fire out of a bush; he looked, and the bush was blazing, yet it was not consumed. Then Moses said, "I must turn

aside and look at this great sight, and see why the bush is not burned up." When the LORD saw that he had turned aside to see, God called to him out of the bush, "Moses, Moses!" And he said, "Here I am." Then he said, "Come no closer! Remove the sandals from your feet, for the place on which you are standing is holy ground."
—*Exodus 3:1–5*

Let him regard all the utensils of the monastery
and its whole property
as if they were the sacred vessels of the altar.
Let him not think that he may neglect anything.
He should be neither a miser
nor a prodigal and squanderer of the monastery's
    substance,
but should do all things with measure
and in accordance with the Abbot's instructions.
—*Rule of Benedict 31*

Now is the time for the world to know
That every thought and action is sacred.
This is the time for you to compute the impossibility
That there is anything
But Grace.

Now is the season to know
That everything you do
Is sacred.
—*Hafiz, "Now Is the Time"*[5]

Every day is a god, each day is a god, and holiness holds forth in time. I worship each god, I praise each day splintered down, splintered down and wrapped in time like a husk, a husk of many colors spreading, at dawn fast over the mountains split.

I open my eyes. The god lifts from the water. His head fills the bay. He is Puget Sound, the Pacific; his breast rises from pastures; his fingers are firs; islands slide wet down his shoulders…. This is the one world, bound to itself and exultant. It fizzes up in trees, trees heaving up streams of salt to their leaves. This is the one air, bitten by grackles; time is alone and in and out of mind. The god of today is a boy, pagan and fernfoot. His power is enthusiasm; his innocence is mystery.

—*Annie Dillard*, Holy the Firm[6]

For Reflection

What are some of the most unforgettable books, poetry, short stories, and articles you have read? What makes them unforgettable?

How have you encountered the most influential material you've read—assignment/obligation? Suggestions from friends or family? General interest? Browsing a bookstore?

At what times in your life have you been most affected by something you've read?

Do you have a favorite word or phrase that you like to see in text or to hear? What draws you to that particular word or phrase?

PART TWO

The Four Movements of *Lectio Divina*

LISTENING FOR GOD'S VOICE

Lectio's Call to Awaken to the Divine

Poets live with silence:
the silence before the poem;
the silence whence the poem comes;

the silence in between the words, as you
drink the words, watch them glide through your mind,
feel them slide down your throat
towards your heart....
—Michael Shepherd, *"Rumi's Silence"*

The first movement of *lectio divina* in traditional language is called *lectio*, which means "reading." But this kind of reading is so much more than simply reading words, stringing together sounds, and comprehending the meaning of those sounds. Rather, the first movement of *lectio* is an entry to awakening your body, mind, and heart to God's presence, listening for God's voice not merely on the surface of the words and phrases, but between them, around them, and deeply within them. In Jewish tradition there is the belief that Torah is black fire on white fire. As Rabbi Avi Weiss writes, "The black letters represent thoughts which are intellectual in nature.... The white spaces, on the other hand, represent that which goes beyond the world of the intellect. The black letters are limited, limiting and fixed. The white spaces catapult us into the realm of the limitless and the ever-changing, ever-growing. They are the story, the song, the silence."[1]

Lectio is something like this, reading the black letters of the sacred text and allowing those to invite us into the deeper mystery of the white spaces in between. In this first movement, you read your selected passage slowly, deliberately, and repeatedly, listening for God's voice to emerge from the words and shimmer within you.

REVERENTIAL LISTENING

> *The disciple's ear, open and attentive, can hear God speaking in the bus-queue, in the supermarket, in the conversation of a tiresomely boring or demanding person, and know instinctively how to respond. That is the supreme spiritual art. Haven't you learned it yet? Of course you haven't. It takes a lifetime to learn it.*
>
> —*Cyprian Smith, OSB*, The Path of Life

While sacred or divine reading is the traditional way of defining *lectio divina*, another phrase that reveals a more substantial dimension of this practice is "reverential listening." In this first movement of *lectio* especially, we begin to attune our ears to the sound of God in our lives. Reverence honors the otherness of God, which prompts us to quiet ourselves to receive Mystery. The practice of *lectio divina* assumes a God who is active and present to us across time and who can speak through texts, even those written hundreds or thousands of years ago. It assumes a God who is already calling to us from these texts and who offers us a gift each time we make room to receive this presence.

When we show reverence, we recognize a presence much more expansive than ourselves at work. It is a response to all the ways God whispers to us through the world. The word is present to us in Scripture, but also in the book of Nature and in the sacred texts of our daily lives. When we reverence something, we wrap our hearts around it and allow it to become enfleshed within us. This practice of reverence is a way of approaching the texts in a manner where we are open to the possibility that they have something to teach us. Reverence is an ever-deepening and awe-filled encounter with the Sacred Presence. It honors words as holy and as revelatory.

Practicing *lectio divina* calls us to an act of resistance against "productivity." When we listen with reverence we are not trying to get anywhere—to the end of the passage or to a particular experience. In a world where everything has a purpose and is to be done efficiently, where we set goals and live by our day-planners telling us the next place to be, *lectio* invites us into a space where we release that compulsiveness. We enter into a kind of slow time, where we touch the eternal moment by bringing ourselves fully present. Eternity isn't to be found elsewhere, or at the end of our days, but is embedded in our daily experience. We have all had moments when we were so immersed in something that we lost track of time. In *lectio* we cultivate this ability to touch the eternal, to open our hearts to a quality of timelessness where agendas and "to do" lists have no place. We are called by this practice to "waste time" in a world that values productivity above all else.

One of my students describes it this way:

Jesus tells us that the Kingdom of Heaven is within. It is not somewhere out there, beyond where we stand right now, nor is it some indeterminate place we shall enter when we die. No, it is here, right here, right now. In the Eternal Now which resides along the vertical axis of our being, and where we hope all our various spiritual practices, *lectio divina* being one, will carry us. (Edith O'Nuallain)

In our culture we are often so focused on getting somewhere or achieving something that we neglect this kind of deep listening in which we access the eternal moment. Life becomes more expansive and we discover the layers of possibility present to us. In *The Sacred Art of Listening*, Kay Lindahl describes listening as a creative force:

> Something quite wonderful occurs when we are listened to fully. We expand, ideas come to life and grow, we remember who we are. Some speak of this force as a creative fountain within us that springs forth; others call it the inner spirit, intelligence, true self. Whatever this force is called, it shrivels up when we are not listened to and it thrives when we are.
>
> The way we listen can actually allow the other person to bring forth what is true and alive to them.[2]

Lectio calls us to cultivate this reverential listening with the text and with the whole of our lives. Listening requires that we have patience and release our expectations of what will happen or our goals to get to a particular point. When we pray *lectio*, we are invited into a different way of being in the world, one that nurtures our ability to be more present in our daily lives.

AWAKENING THE BODY, MIND, AND HEART

The first movement of *lectio* call us to awaken our bodies, minds, and hearts to the present moment, to the words of our selected passage, and to God's presence embedded within them and around us. In his prologue to the Rule, Benedict quotes Paul's letter to the Romans: "It is high time for us to arise from sleep." There are many invitations in both the Hebrew and the Christian scriptures to awaken to the presence of God in our midst and not be tempted to go back to sleep. In the story of the call of Samuel (1 Kings 3:1–21), God awakens Samuel from sleep to follow him and become a prophet to the Israelites. One of the most poignant examples of this is the story of Jesus in the Garden of Gethsemane (Luke 22:39–46), at the foot of the Mount of Olives. On the night before his crucifixion, Jesus gathers his disciples with him for a final meal. He knows the fate awaiting him, and so after they eat he asks the disciples to stay awake with him and pray. They are unable, perhaps because of too much food and wine or, more likely, their own resistance to being fully aware of what is to happen to their beloved companion. Luke says that Jesus "found them sleeping because of grief." Jesus then calls the disciples to awaken and stay alert. When we resist the truth of our experience, we fall asleep to what is most real. In our *lectio divina* practice we are being invited to wake up and stay alert, to make room for what is happening within us.

When our bodies and our senses are awakened, we begin to become aware of places in our lives where we have become hard-hearted. The Hebrew scriptures call us to move from a heart of stone to a heart of flesh, as God said to the prophet Ezekiel, "A new heart I will give you, and a new spirit I will put within you; and I will remove from your body the heart of stone and give you a heart of flesh" (Ezekiel 36:26). We harden so many parts of ourselves to protect us from pain or disappointment, automatically tightening our stomach muscles when anticipating a blow to the belly, or bracing our arms to block a fall or flying object. We harden our bodies without realizing it, involuntarily clenching parts of ourselves such as our jaws or fists, in response to stress.

Like our bodies, our minds can become hardened as well. We become rigid in our thinking about ourselves, such as when we limit future possibilities because of past experiences. Our minds become hardened against other people when we rely on stereotypes or assume we know how someone will respond to us. Sometimes our thoughts become cluttered with self-judgment or resentment toward others, while cynicism and a belief that life is limited to what we can see hardens our minds. *Lectio* helps us awaken to the sacred voice in the text that ultimately speaks across our lives.

THE SACRED ART OF ATTENTION

The ancient monks would read the scriptures very slowly, line by line. After each line they would pause and ponder and allow it to sink into the body. When a particular word or phrase kindled the heart and the imagination, they would rest there and allow the prayer experience to unfold.

This is the sacred art of attention, the intentional act of focusing body, mind, and heart in order to be wholly attentive to subtle movements of energy when we hear a particular word or phrase in the text. This energetic response might feel "positive" in the sense of being attracted to the word or phrase— experiencing a deep resonance, feeling a sense of delight or possibility when first encountering it, recognizing a sense of synchronicity in the way it might be already speaking to your inner experience. However, the energetic response might also feel "negative"; perhaps you will experience a sense of challenge or irritation, discord, or dissonance. The word or phrase might create an unsettled feeling within, or a sense of restlessness. When I pray *lectio* and read over my chosen text, I sometimes find that there is a word or phrase that calls to me in this way, but I resist at first because I want a word that sounds more peaceful or more "hopeful."

This cultivation of attention can help us in our everyday lives as well when we deliberately slow ourselves down, observe our experience, and notice our energetic response to moments. We can become more aware of our responses to life experiences and create internal space to explore the feeling. How often we move quickly through life without giving pause and noticing how we actually are responding to a given moment. *Lectio* calls us to be present to this inner experience without judgment, and to respond to these energetic "shimmerings" within as an invitation into the ways God is working in our lives.

Sacred texts speak to our hearts in the here and now of our lives. Our *lectio* practice cultivates a sense of inner peace, movement on the spiritual path, and growth toward accepting who we are most called to be. But Scripture also challenges us and calls us to wrestle with it. Spirituality isn't meant to be all sweetness and light. In fact, genuine maturity only comes from allowing life's inevitable difficulties to soften us and bring us to a place of greater compassion. Contemplative practice is in service to this process. I often call to mind the story in Genesis 32 of Jacob wrestling with an angel all night long. Jacob does not let the angel go until he is given a blessing. His blessing is a new name, Israel, "for you have striven with God and with humans, and have prevailed" (32:28). While wrestling, Jacob's hip is wounded and so he walks with a limp for the rest of his life. This is often how our lives are: we have an experience that shakes us, challenges us, or upends our core beliefs. We may feel like we have wrestled with an angel all night. Yet the spiritual journey calls us to actively engage with God even if we are wounded in the process. Blessings and curses often enter our lives together, and growth in spiritual depth, wisdom, and maturity lies in the ability to embrace the paradoxes and tensions of life.

So as you listen for the word or phrase, you are opening yourself to unexplored areas that may stir difficult feelings. Most often these are the places that also need healing. When we avoid these feelings we tend to project them onto other people instead, or else the resistance comes out in other ways. Think of this as an intuitive process of becoming more present to your immediate experience, rather than merely thinking through which word or phrase would be most valuable for you to focus on. As you listen, see if you can release thoughts and respond from a heart-centered place.

ASCETICISM, SIMPLICITY, AND THE PRACTICE OF LETTING GO

> *Much of spiritual practice is just this: cutting away*
> *what must be cut, and letting remain what must*
> *remain. Knowing what to cut—this is wisdom.*
> *Being clear and strong enough to make the cut when*
> *it is time for things to go—this is courage. Together,*
> *the practices of wisdom and courage enable us, day*
> *by day, task by task, to gradually simplify our life.*
> —Wayne Muller, How, Then, Shall We Live?

In monasticism, a great deal of emphasis is placed on asceticism, the practice of releasing what is not necessary. In our own prayer, we do well to follow this call of simplicity. The practice of asceticism is to let go of material things we do not need, but also to release ideas about ourselves and others, including judgments and expectations that no longer serve us.

The call of *lectio divina* is into the deep heart of prayer, where there is only one thing necessary—a loving encounter with the Source of all creation. It is a lifelong journey to learn this path of simplicity in our prayer as well as our external lives. Asceticism is about becoming conscious of the habits that keep us from a sustained gaze upon the Holy One, and working to eliminate those distractions from our lives. As we enter into the first movement of *lectio*, the invitation is to release these patterns of behavior and notice our longing to do something else or be somewhere else. It is the simple letting go of our own sense of achievement and entering into the unadorned truth of what this moment has to offer. Camaldolese monk Cyprian Consiglio tells the story of Fr. Bede Griffiths, one of the great spiritual leaders of the twentieth century, who admonished one of his students that God is not an object of prayer. The *subject* of prayer is God; the purpose of prayer is not so much to make contact with God, but "to remove everything that prevents you from listening to God speaking in you."[3] In ascetic practice we strive to release even the ideas we have of God and allow God to come unbidden, new and fresh. This is how we enter into our *lectio divina*. The purpose of contemplative practice is to cultivate inner and outer freedom so that we can respond more authentically to each moment and each invitation. We can be attached to such subtle things as set spiritual practices, certain doctrines, or a particular experience of consolation, all of which can stand in the way of experiencing the truth of the moment. In the first movement of *lectio* we establish our desire to free ourselves from whatever might hinder our presence to the experience. Consider the subtle things in your life that get in the way of your ability to be truly present and to respond authentically in prayer. Remember that this is a lifelong journey.

Invitation to Practice: Shimmering

He does not always remain bent over his pages;
he often leans back and closes his eyes over a
line he has been reading again, and its meaning
spreads through his blood.
—Rainer Maria Rilke, The Notebooks of
Malte Laurids Brigge

Now we will explore the first movement of *lectio divina* more deeply. There are also some suggestions at the end for other ways to enter into the word or phrase that rises up in your prayer.

Begin by selecting a passage for prayer and putting it to one side. It might be one from the end of this chapter.

Settling

Leading into the first movement is your time of preparation, when you turn off the phone, close the door, set aside distractions, and step apart from the world for a brief while. This is all part of the process of settling into the experience. Practice simplicity by letting go of whatever is not needed right now. Rituals help signal to the body and spirit that something holy is happening. Lighting a candle, saying a blessing, and closing your eyes to pause and gather your awareness are all powerful aspects of how we might enter into prayer. Benedict writes in the Rule: "First of all, every time you begin a good work, you must pray to God most earnestly to bring it to perfection" (Prologue: 3). The intentionality with which you make the transition into prayer will assist the deepening of your practice.

As you settle into your prayer experience, allow some extra time to slow yourself down. You want to experience the fullness of this first movement of *lectio divina* as much as possible, even if that means you only focus on a small portion of your selected passage. But as we already have discovered, since we aren't trying to "get anywhere," whatever happens will be more than enough.

Sink into your chair and allow some time to simply be present to your body's experience. Notice all the places your body is in contact with the chair and the ground. Offer a moment of gratitude for all the ways you are supported right now: for the gift of a chair to keep your body upright, for the holy ground beneath your feet, for the gift of time to be able simply to be and notice. If you are aware of any places of tension in your body, shift in any way that might help ease the tension. Cultivate your sense of attention to all of these elements.

The moments of preparation for contemplative prayer are important to the integrity of the practice. Create both space and time, become aware of our intention for the practice, and hold a spirit of openness to what might happen. Beginning this time with a prayer or blessing and connection to the breath helps us shift to a receiving space.

Transitions into prayer help to indicate to ourselves how much we honor and value this commitment. In our culture we rush so often from one thing to another. Both the time we enter and the time we depart this prayer space should be slow and focused. In yoga practice we are encouraged to be present to how we come into and come out of a physical pose—the attentiveness is not just for the time we hold the pose itself, but also for before and after. When our movement between places and experiences can also be infused with awareness, we can grow in our ability to remain aware when life forces us into change we didn't choose or anticipate. We can practice this presence as we move into and out of prayer.

Now become aware of your breath, aware of the rhythm of inhale and exhale that sustains you moment by moment. Offer gratitude for this most elemental and essential gift of breath. As you breathe in, imagine the source of all breath breathing life into you, enlivening you. As you breathe out, allow yourself to release whatever the rest of the day holds and any thoughts you might have of future obligations and responsibilities. Bring yourself fully into the present now.

Breathe in the gift of peace, breathe out and release any expectations you have for what this time of prayer holds. Breathe in the gift of silence, breathe out and release any compulsion you might be experiencing to "get somewhere" in your prayer. Breathe in the gift of being, breathe out and release the need to do anything, letting go of the busyness of the world. Breathe in love, breathe out judgments that may emerge concerning what you should or should not be doing. Just allow whatever your experience is in this moment to have its space.

Be aware of thoughts that will inevitably rise up in your mind. As they do, simply notice them and release them gently with the exhalation. With each breath you take, settle yourself more deeply into this moment and bring your full presence here, right now.

As you settle into the rhythm of your breath, begin to gently draw your awareness from your head down to your heart center. You might even place your hand over your heart to create a physical connection and feel the rise and fall of your breath and the beating of your heart as the two primal rhythms of life.

As you bring your awareness to your heart, entering this inner sanctuary, imagine that you are passing through a doorway that leads into the heart of God. Spend a few moments simply resting here, feeling whatever the truth of your experience is in this moment, allowing it to have space.

Then bring to your awareness what the scriptures and mystics tell us, the infinite compassion of God that dwells within your heart. Breathe in this infinite source of compassion and allow it to fill you. Breathe out, surrendering more deeply into this moment.

From this heart-centered space, offer a commitment to reverential listening for this time ahead. Consider a gesture that evokes this for you—perhaps your hands in prayer position or open in your lap as a way to receive whatever comes in this time ahead.

Shimmering

Now read your selected text very slowly. Read the words aloud and taste them on your tongue. Notice how each one feels in your mouth. Read the selection at least twice. Receive the words of the sacred text as if they were a love letter written from God to you in this very moment of your life. Imagine that there are seeds in this passage that respond to your own deepest longings, the ones perhaps that you haven't yet even named.

As you read the words of your selected passage aloud and really hear them, practice reverential listening for a word or phrase that chooses you. Notice if one of the words or phrases creates an energetic response within you. This could be a positive response or one where you experience resistance. Trust that the energy stirred in you has some wisdom to offer.

Pause and let the words of your selected passage echo within your heart. As you stay present to the text, is there a word or phrase that feels like it is shimmering right now? Is there a word or phrase that is in some way choosing you, or unnerving you, or challenging you? Try not to think this through, but just allow yourself to trust your intuitive response. If judgments arise, return to the breath, becoming present again to your heart.

As the word or phrase becomes clearer, gently repeat it to yourself again and again. Try saying it differ- ent ways or even singing the word or phrase aloud.

From here you can choose to continue the rest of the movements of *lectio divina* (refer back to Chapter Two for an outline of the whole experience), or you might consider trying out one of the following suggestions.

Further Possibilities for Practice

Using a Mantra

The Sanskrit word *mantra* combines the root word *man* (to think) with the suffix *tra* (instrument or tool). Mantra means an "instrument for thought," or a tool that helps guide our thoughts.

If you practice *lectio divina* in the morning, consider writing your word or phrase down on a small card such as an index card and keeping it in your pocket or wallet. Allow it to be your mantra for the rest of the day, a holy word or phrase that calls your focus back to the present moment. Pray with it throughout the day. Memorize it and allow it to rise up again and again. Repeat it as often as you can remember.

Synchronicity

As you pray with the word throughout the day, listen for any meaningful coincidences that occur. When you pray with a text and it works its way into your heart, you may discover that you begin to see the image appearing many places in different guises. Listening for this kind of synchronicity is a way of paying attention to the deep hum of the world in harmony with your prayer.

Writing

Take some paper and colored markers. Write the word or phrase from your prayer again and again in different colors and in different kinds of handwriting—script, block print, scribble, flowery. Allow the words to overlap one another. You don't have to be a calligrapher to experience the joy of writing as meditative practice. As you write each word, allow it to have a moment of echo in your heart. Notice how the act of writing the words brings you into more intimacy with them.

Poetry Exploration: Haiku

After each time of prayer, consider writing a poem in haiku in response to your experience. There is something powerful about distilling your experience into seventeen syllables. Traditionally haiku is written with the first line containing five syllables, seven syllables in the second line, and five syllables again in the third line. However, in

the Japanese language there is even greater compact-
ness of expression, so feel free to write even fewer words
to express the essence of your prayer.

In her book *Haiku: A Spiritual Practice in Three Lines*,
Margaret McGee suggests allowing the practice of *lectio
divina* to be an inspiration for writing haiku. She writes
her haiku on a sticky note or bookmark that she then
keeps with the original text so when she goes back she
has a connection to her experience again in this way.[4] To
give you an example of the practice, here are some
verses of haiku written by some of my workshop participants in response to their experience of *lectio divina*.
One woman wrote this haiku in response to the Scripture
passage from Matthew 6:21, "For where your treasure is,
there your heart will be also."

> Love's alchemy
> my heart's transformation
> What priceless treasure. (Cheryl Macpherson)

Another participant was captured by the verse from
Isaiah about the word of God being sent out into the
world, focusing on the phrase, "it shall not return to me
empty" (55:11). She said, "Perhaps because I have been
feeling so drained and so empty lately. 'Soul dry' is a
phrase that keeps popping into my head":

> Breathing out I know
> that which I breathe in is Source
> —I am not empty. (Eveline Maedel)

Suggested Texts for *Lectio Divina*: Listening

He said, "Go out and stand on the mountain
before God, for God is about to pass by." Now

there was a great wind, so strong that it was
splitting mountains and breaking rocks in pieces
before God, but God was not in the wind; and
after the wind an earthquake, but God was not in
the earthquake; and after the earthquake a fire,
but God was not in the fire; and after the fire a
sound of sheer silence. When Elijah heard it, he
wrapped his face in his mantle and went out and
stood at the entrance of the cave.

—*1 Kings 19:11–13a*

My child, be attentive to my words;
incline your ear to my sayings.
Do not let them escape from your sight;
keep them within your heart.
For they are life to those who find them,
and healing to all their flesh.
Keep your heart with all vigilance,
for from it flow the springs of life.

—*Proverbs 4:20–23*

The Lord GOD has given me
the tongue of a teacher,
that I may know how to sustain
the weary with a word.
Morning by morning he wakens—
wakens my ear
to listen as those who are taught.
The Lord GOD has opened my ear,
and I was not rebellious,
I did not turn backwards.

—*Isaiah 50:4–5*

Listen! A sower went out to sow. And as he
sowed, some seeds fell on the path, and the

birds came and ate them up. Other seeds fell on rocky ground, where they did not have much soil, and they sprang up quickly, since they had no depth of soil. But when the sun rose, they were scorched; and since they had no root, they withered away. Other seeds fell among thorns, and the thorns grew up and choked them. Other seeds fell on good soil and brought forth grain, some a hundredfold, some sixty, some thirty. Let anyone with ears listen!

—*Matthew 13:3–9*

Let us get up then, at long last, for the Scriptures rouse us when they say: *It is high time for us to arise from sleep* (Romans 13:11). Let us open our eyes to the light that comes from God, and our ears to the voice from heaven that every day calls out this charge: *If today you hear God's voice, do not harden your hearts* (Psalm 94:8). And again: *You that have ears to hear, listen to what the Spirit says to the churches* (Revelation 2:7).

—*Rule of Benedict, Prologue 9–11*

For Reflection

What are the ideas you have about yourself that get in the way of prayer and your relationship with God?

How are you being invited into a greater sense of simplicity in your life and prayer?

What are the biggest challenges for you in resting in the space of not-doing? Of waiting? Of resting? Of being nonproductive?

What are the ways you seek to control time?

What are the ways you avoid the messiness of life? By doing so, what do you think you are missing? What do you think you are gaining?

CHAPTER SIX

SAVORING SACRED TEXT

Meditatio's Welcoming with All Senses

Meditation moves from looking at the words of the text to entering the world of the text. As we take this text into ourselves, we find that the text is taking us into itself. For the world of the text is far larger and more real than our minds and experience.... This text is God-revealing: God creating, God saving, God blessing.... There is always more to anything, any word or sentence, than meets the eye; meditation enters into the large backgrounds that are not immediately visible, that we overlooked the first time around.
—*Eugene Peterson*, Eat This Book: A Conversation in the Art of Spiritual Reading

In the previous chapter I focused on *lectio*, the first movement of *lectio divina*, which includes the dynamics of settling and shimmering—preparing yourself to enter the deep silence of the heart and then listen for the word or phrase from the sacred text that chooses you, calls to you, asks for your attention. In this chapter I move into the second movement, traditionally called *meditatio* in Latin, or meditation. In *meditatio*, you allow the word or phrase that has settled in your heart to unfold within you. You savor it, inviting in the images and feelings it conjures for you.

PRAYING WITH THE SENSES

> *But a person has within himself three paths: What*
> *are they? The soul, the body, and the senses; and all*
> *human life is led in these. How? The soul vivifies*
> *the body and conveys the breath of life to the senses;*
> *the body draws the soul to itself and opens the senses;*
> *and the senses touch the soul and draw the body.*
> —Hildegard of Bingen, Scivias

The second movement of *lectio divina* is in part an invitation to savor. The word *savor* comes from the Latin word *sapere*, meaning "to know," and is the root of the Latin word for wisdom, *sapientia*. In this way savoring and wisdom are connected at their root meaning. We don't gain wisdom by rushing through life and skimming across its surface, but by going slowly and diving deeply. Savoring engages all of our senses. Think of a time when you sat down to a beautiful meal and the smells and tastes evoked in you a sense of spaciousness. We live in a culture that does not promote experiences like this. Instead, we are encouraged to rush through our tasks, to do it all, to experience as much as possible. We eat "fast food" in an effort to quickly satisfy our hunger, for example, but we end up suffering from undernourishment because we miss the soulful experience of eating a meal.

Savoring implies lingering with the experience; in that sense, it is the opposite of consumption. We are invited to enter into the sacred text and linger there for the full sense experience of what we are offered. The sixteenth-century Spanish mystic Ignatius of Loyola encouraged such savoring through what he called the prayer of the imagination. With this kind of prayer we don't simply read through a scriptural passage; we are also asked to imagine ourselves in the scene that the passage depicts. Through our imagination we step into the actual scene portrayed in the passage and tend to the full sensory experience we encounter there. We are called upon to hear the voices and sounds around us, to smell the dust or dew, to taste the bread and wine, to see everything around us. Ignatius lived several centuries after *lectio divina* was developed and would certainly have been familiar with this way of praying. In many ways, prayer of the imagination is a deeply expanded version of *meditatio*.

In *Eat This Book*, Eugene Peterson presents an image of moving from the words of the text to the world of the text. We move the words into our hearts and allow them to be broken open. Imagine the first new bud of spring and its moment of bursting open in vibrant color and fragrance, and how this experience is always greater than what we anticipated. Or remember a time when you opened a jar of perfumed oil or honey and allowed the contents to pour forth, filling the air with its aroma. I remember an amaryllis bulb I received as a gift one spring. It arrived with its petals closed tightly, but in the morning they had spread wide in a display of crimson velvet. And while I had seen an open amaryllis before, this moment of receiving the blooming of life anew was sheer gift. This is what the unfolding of the word or phrase in *meditatio* can be like.

The first step of *lectio divina* is settling into the stillness and becoming fully present, moving our awareness into our hearts. This is all part of preparing ourselves for the second step, which is the experience of savoring. We slow ourselves down so that when the word or phrase plants itself in our heart's awareness, we can create enough space around it to allow it to fully flower. When we enter into the wide open space of our hearts and imaginations, we give room for connections to emerge, to notice the resonances this word or phrase has with our own experience. There is a spirit of playfulness that is set free as we enter into the text with openness. When we "play" with the words, we allow ourselves to stretch beyond our own assumptions and rules about what something means. There is a wide expanse within every sacred text awaiting our willingness to meet it and be enlarged by it, to step into its landscape and hold our hearts open in wonder. As we ponder and savor the word or phrase, images or feelings arise. A memory stirs in our awareness, perhaps something we haven't thought about in a long while, and we take the time to wonder where it came from.

The idea of *meditatio* is to make space within us to allow the free form of possibilities without making judgments that cut them off. Our analyzing mind often wants to cut off the imaginings, judging them as silly, or trying to fit them into the box of our previous understandings. But the way we enter into relationship with poetry and art is not with analysis but by yielding our hearts, opening our intuition, discovering new symbols, and cultivating artistic appreciation. *Meditatio* is the art of savoring. As Guigo expresses in his *Ladder of Monks*,

> I have long meditated in my heart and in my meditation a fire grew with a desire to know you more. While you broke the bread of sacred scripture for me you have become known to me in the breaking of the bread. The more I know you, the more I long to know you, no longer in the husks of the letter but in the senses of experience.

The second movement of *lectio divina* cultivates our intuitive sense and ability to hold paradox in tension. *Meditatio* moves us to release our thinking mind with its dualities of either/or and to rest in intutive and sensual experience as a window to the sacred. As we engage our senses, we discover new dimensions of the text because the experience of smell, taste, and sound have different kinds of logic than do words and thinking.

INNER HOSPITALITY: WELCOMING BOTH GIFTS AND GRIEF

> *The virgin point within the heart is like a pure dia-*
> *mond blazing with the invisible light of heaven. It is*
> *in everybody. And if we could see it we would see*
> *these billions of points of light coming together in*
> *the face and blaze of a sun that would make all the*
> *darkness and cruelty of life vanish completely ... the*
> *Gate of Heaven is everywhere.*
>
> —*Thomas Merton*, Conjectures of a
> Guilty Bystander

Hospitality is a sacred art in many faith traditions. In Judaism, it is considered a *mitzvah*, or commandment. The first time we encounter hospitality in the Hebrew scriptures is in the book of Genesis, when Abraham welcomes three strangers by the oaks of Mamre, who reward his generosity by telling him that his aged wife Sarah will bear a son. The Christian scriptures' letter to the Hebrews refers back to Abraham's story when it urges generosity: "Do not neglect to show hospitality to strangers, for by doing that some have entertained angels without knowing it" (Hebrews 13:2). This ideal of hospitality is reinforced in the Rule of Benedict: "All guests who present themselves are to be welcome as Christ" (53:1). It has largely to do with how we encounter strangers, not just friends and loved ones. In Islam, the hospitality relationship is triangular, including host, stranger, and God. Sustenance is a right rather than a gift, and the obligation is to God, not merely to the stranger.

In *Hospitality: The Sacred Art*, Nanette Sawyer describes the practice of hospitality as beginning with receptivity as a posture of invitation, openness, and possibility. She next describes hospitality as moving to reverence as a posture of welcome:

To welcome deeply means to encounter the fullness of a person, perceive his or her inherent integrity and intrinsic value, and then engage it with your full self. Reverence says, I value who you are and what you have to offer to me, to us (you and me), and to the world. In a state of reverence, we stand in the full presence of another, while being fully present ourselves. There is deep acceptance and love in this state, as we encounter the image of God in each other.

Finally, a spirit of generosity allows us to give ourselves fully over to this experience. Generosity is a posture of nurture in which the abundance of life is affirmed:

> This abundance is not related to how many possessions we have; rather, it's about living life in all its fullness—*abundant life*. Suddenly we realize that we have much more than we understood ourselves to have. We begin to realize that what we actually *need* in human life is a lot less stuff and a lot more relationship.[1]

In this second movement of *lectio divina*, we practice a kind of inner hospitality. We make room within ourselves to savor and allow images, feelings, and memories to stir within our hearts and rise up to our awareness. Through our own inner capacities for hospitality, we open ourselves to receive, welcome, and nurture these gifts of contemplative prayer.

What we feel and experience in *lectio divina* won't always be pleasant or full of delight. Sometimes the feelings that rise up include sorrow, grief, and anger; at other times we may also experience dryness and desolation in prayer. These are experiences we typically want to resist, but when we do, we either deny their existence within us or rush to be in a more comfortable place. For example, as a culture we strongly discourage people who are grieving to stay with their sadness, but instead tell them to "cheer up" or "move on" rather than explore what grief has to teach them. Yet developing the capacity to endure and remain open to difficult feelings is part of the movement toward spiritual maturity.

To help us avoid such resistance we must cultivate our "inner witness," that part of ourselves that lets us experience what saddens, angers, or challenges us without getting carried away by emotions. The concept of inner witness or internal observer goes by different names in different spiritual traditions. The Sanskrit word is *sakshi*—*sa* means "with" and *aksha* means "senses" or "eyes." Thus, *sakshi* is the capacity each of us holds to disengage from identification with our thoughts, and at the same time, observe them "with our eyes." In other words, we can witness the operations of our mind directly and yet cultivate our ability to stay detached from them. My own practice of yoga has been a profound teacher for me of learning how to stay present with discomfort. I favor *yin* yoga, in which the poses are held for longer periods of time, than *yang*, or active practice. It allows me to develop the skill of observing my own edges, the places where judgments rise up in my mind, and the ways I hold tension in my body.

The twentieth-century monk and poet Thomas Merton drew from the Sufis to describe the *point vierge*—the "virgin point" of the soul—the part of ourselves deep within the heart that is untouched by our daily fears and anxieties, the place in which God dwells. This inner witness is our calm core, the place within us of infinite compassion and curiosity about our experience. When we move into silence and we begin to notice the inner voices rising up, it is our inner witness that can observe this dialogue without getting caught up in the emotional drama of it. Cultivating an awareness of this dimension takes practice. We enter into contemplative ways of praying to access this brilliance within us, to rest into our own hearts and discover there the heart of God. When making the space within ourselves to experience the full range of what wants to move and open, we also make room for the difficult and challenging aspects of our humanity.

The Rule of Benedict instructs that all are to welcome in the stranger at the door and greet that stranger knowing that Christ is present. There is deep wisdom here for us to ponder. In our meditation practice, we are similarly called upon to welcome the strangers knocking at the inner door of our hearts and see the presence of the Holy there. We are able to do this because we have within us an inner witness, a virgin point, that remains steadfast and is not carried away by emotions. We have the capacity to allow in the full spectrum of our emotions and thereby grow in wisdom by staying present to them.

The inner witness is able to notice whatever feeling is arising and can also be curious about it. What is this about for me? Why am I experiencing this now? What does the inner landscape of this emotion look like? Our meditation becomes a lens through which we can begin to observe the patterns of our thoughts in daily life. The resistance that emerges in prayer is the same that comes up in our response to relationships. For example, if while observing my thoughts I notice that I am full of judgment about how I am not doing it "right," I might become curious as to where else in my life this tendency to criticize myself and others appears. Cultivating inner awareness helps us grow in freedom as we begin to see ourselves more clearly. The inner witness is rooted in the infinite compassion of God and can hold our own vulnerability with great tenderness and understanding. When we are unable to be compassionate with ourselves, we are usually unable to accept the shortcomings of others.

Buddhist monk Thich Nhat Hanh speaks of this ability to witness oneself with compassion while experiencing difficult feelings:

> The Buddhist attitude is to take care of anger. We don't
> suppress it. We don't run away from it. We just breathe

and hold our anger in our arms with utmost tenderness. Becoming angry at your anger only doubles it and makes you suffer more.

The important thing is to bring out the awareness of your anger to protect and sponsor it. Then the anger is no longer alone; it is with your mindfulness. Anger is like a closed flower in the morning. As the bright sun shines on the flower, the flower will bloom because the sunlight penetrates deep into the flower.

Mindfulness is like that. If you keep breathing and sponsoring your anger, mindfulness particles will infiltrate the anger. When sunshine penetrates a flower, the flower cannot resist. It is bound to open itself and reveal its heart to the sun. If you keep breathing on your anger, shining your compassion and understanding on it, your anger will soon crack and you will be able to look into its depths and see its roots.[2]

Mindfulness in Buddhist tradition is similar to the qualitities of awareness, attentiveness, and presence that we cultivate in *meditatio* and Christian prayer. When we bring ourselves fully into the moment, we can become more receptive to the feelings we experience without judging them, without being carried away by their power. Thich Nhat Hanh is writing about anger, but he could be speaking about any of the difficult emotions. We are called to bring compassion to the full spectrum of our inner responses to life.

The breath is an important aspect of this work. Our breath helps us be present, relax the body, and open up space within us to do this vital work. When we resist our inner experience and the emotions that accompany them, the feelings become stuck in our bodies. We live in a culture that doesn't honor difficult feelings, where we are encouraged to shortcut our grief and "move on with things." When we enter meditation, however, we give ourselves space in which to experience them. The more we develop this inner witness aspect of ourselves, the more we are able to meet and better understand ourselves. It brings compassion to whatever we are feeling, and welcomes it in as a source of wisdom for understanding ourselves better.

As you continue to practice your *lectio divina*, see if you can access this "wise witness" part of yourself and welcome in the feelings that move through you. Emotions have energy; when we resist them, they become trapped in us and end up being expressed in other, often unconscious ways. Suppressed grief might emerge as anger in an unexpected moment, for example, and we will find ourselves carried away by the feeling.

When we give emotions room to flow, rather than bottling them up, we find they often dissipate again. They ebb and flow like waves. We can become curious about our emotions and notice when grief, anger, boredom, joy, or another emotion appears, asking what it might have to teach us about our inner life right now. In this movement of awareness toward the feelings that are stirred in our response to a sacred text, we may be called upon to go places we wouldn't have gone intentionally or willingly. In this practice we become present to the places of resistance, and we gently soften ourselves—bodies, minds, hearts—when we become conscious of the ways we resist our own deeply held experiences.

A PLACE FOR PRAISE AND LAMENT

> *Give your sorrow all the space and shelter in yourself that is its due, for if everyone bears his grief honestly and courageously, the sorrow that now fills the world will abate.*
>
> —*Etty Hillesum*, An Interrupted Life

The practice of *meditatio* calls us to welcome in and make room for the full spectrum of who we are. Through this process we remember all the parts of ourselves; we are made whole again. We make this kind of space to explore difficult feelings to bring the wholeness of who we are into prayer. Prayer is not just about finding happiness—although certainly joy is often a fruit of prayer—but also about allowing the full range of ourselves to have voice. We often resist our grief and may find freedom in the sacred tradition of lament.

The book of Lamentations is traditionally ascribed to the prophet Jeremiah following the destruction of Jerusalem and the Temple in 586 BCE. In the Hebrew Bible it is called *Ekah,* meaning "How," which is the first word of the text and the formula to begin a song of wailing: "How lonely sits the city that was once full of people!" The Hebrew scriptures are filled with these songs of wailing—deep expressions of grief, anger, and helplessness. As you pray with difficult texts, notice the feelings that stir in you and make space for them. Remember that emotions are a form of energy that will move through the body when we welcome them in and breathe deeply. From the perspective of the inner witness we can be present to the landscape of grief and "know sorrow as the deepest thing," as the poet Naomi Shahab Nye writes, without being swept away by it. We grow in compassion when we can honor the song of wailing that dwells within each of us.

In the Hebrew Bible we encounter the full range of human emotion as well. The psalms offer us the entire spectrum of human experience uttered in the context of prayer. The psalms of gratitude and praise are full of joy and the language of delight. They celebrate the ways God is visibly at work in the world— through creation and the abundance of God's other gifts offered each day. For example, Psalm 98 urges, "Make a joyful noise to the Lord, all the earth; break forth into joyous song and sing praises. Sing praises to the Lord with the lyre, with the lyre and the sound of melody" (verses 4–5), and Psalm 104 begins: "Bless the Lord, O my soul. O Lord my God, you are very great. You are clothed with honor and majesty, wrapped in light as with a garment" (verses 1–2).

The psalms of lament, however, can be much more challenging to read. Some of the language is more violent and difficult to bear, especially in the context of prayer. And yet there is great wisdom in these words that express the full range of our humanity. Have you ever cried your own version of "My God, my God, why have you forsaken me?" (Psalm 22:1) in a moment of despair? Or asked, "How long, O Lord? Will you forget me forever? How long will you hide your face from me? How long must I bear pain in my soul, and have sorrow in my heart all day long?" (Psalm 13:1–2). The psalmists tell us these longings are to be brought to our prayer. Prayers don't have to be cheerful to be authentic expressions of the heart. If grief stirs in our prayer, we must welcome it with compassion.

Theologian Walter Brueggemann writes about the need for lament in his book *The Prophetic Imagination*. He believes that people can only dare to envision a new reality when they have been able to grieve, to scream out, to let loose the cry that has been stuck in their throats for so long. That cry, the expression of that grief, says Brueggemann, "is the most visceral announcement that things are not right." Only then can we begin to "to nurture, nourish, and evoke a (new) consciousness," a new vision.[3] We so desperately need a new way of seeing the world.

The prayer of lament is first and foremost truth telling. *This* pain, *this* suffering should not be. It helps us name the lies we have been living and participating in. Lament opens us up to a new vision of how God is present to our suffering. We call on the God who weeps with us, whose groans are our own, and we express our hope in God's tender care. These biblical texts offer us a sacred container within which we can experience the full range of our humanness. We are called upon in *lectio divina* to both pray with texts that seem difficult and allow the difficult emotions to rise up within us, even when we weren't expecting them—perhaps especially so.

A participant in one of my classes shares this experience about her experience of grief and *lectio divina*:

I remember many years ago, when my children were babies, and how after their births, I suffered from postnatal depression, one of the symptoms of which was a terrifying fear of setting foot outside the door.

Yet I missed the feel of the wind upon my face, and the warmth of the sun like loving kindness being poured upon me from the heavens above, and so I gathered myself and my little ones up and bundled us all out the front door into the strange, slightly menacing world which lay beyond.

But as I walked, each step hurt. Every person I passed seemed to carry some essence which brushed against my being, bruising my already damaged and hurting soul within. The tears came unbidden and I didn't want either my children or any strangers to see the wetness on my face, and so I walked with my head held low.

And I began to pray. I prayed that She Who I Yearned to Believe In would come and walk beside me. And I called also upon my favorite female saints and mystics and begged them to surround me and to help me not give up, give in, succumb to this barren emptiness which threatened to engulf my soul and my life in its terrifying darkness.

And do you know something? They did come, every one of them.

And how do I know this? I felt them in the fluttering of the hem of my dress and in the sounds of the leaves rustling in the trees, and in the rain that joined me in my tears filled with fear and loss and hope and grace and most of all, Mercy.

And since those days when I did not walk alone, whenever I feel the fingers of darkness begin to creep toward me, I call upon my circle of friends, my saints, my mystics, my very own cohort of women, and they hold my hand and help me get to where I am going.

They always come when I practice *lectio*. (Edith O'Nuallain)

Invitation to Practice: Savoring and Stirring

Now you will explore the second movement of *lectio divina* more deeply through practice. I invite you to pray with a passage from the Song of Songs from the Hebrew scriptures, which overflows with sensual imagery. It is an important text for both Jewish and Christian mystics as a metaphor for the intimacy that God, as Beloved, calls us to:

Your channel is an orchard of pomegranates
with all choicest fruits,
henna with nard,
nard and saffron, calamus and cinnamon,
with all trees of frankincense,
myrrh and aloes,
with all chief spices—
a garden fountain, a well of living water,
and flowing streams from Lebanon.

Awake, O north wind,
and come, O south wind!
Blow upon my garden
that its fragrance may be wafted abroad.
Let my beloved come to his garden,
and eat its choicest fruits.

—*Song of Songs 4:13–16*

Settling and Shimmering

Begin your practice in the usual way of settling into your body and breath. Allow your breath to embrace the presence of God in this moment and release whatever stands in the way, such as your personal expectations or judgments. Allow your awareness to descend from your head into your heart and open yourself up to the experience of reverential listening and receiving the words of a sacred text as a gift. Read through the passage twice, identifying the word or phrase that shimmers today. Then rest for a few moments with it, gently repeating it to yourself.

Savoring

Once you have allowed the word or phrase to choose you, sink into the experience of allowing it to unfold in your imagination. What images are you aware of? Savoring the sacred text means tending to its sights, smells, sounds, tastes, and touch. With each breath, open yourself to the experience being offered to you. Imagine the word or phrase as a tiny sacred seed being planted in the rich and fertile soil of your heart, and this unfolding as a process of beholding what emerges. Allow each inhale to create more inner space within your heart for your intuition and imagination to have freedom.

As you become aware of thoughts, judgments, or expectations, gently release them with your breath. You may find that as images rise up, your thinking mind wants to either dismiss them as unimportant or analyze them to figure out their meaning. Release these tendencies when they come up. Remember that savoring takes time, and you are allowing the full spectrum of possibility to bloom. Allow some silence to surround the images that are forming.

Notice if a memory is beginning to stir, and allow yourself to tend to the experience it evokes. What do you remember about the sense experience of this moment? Allow some silence around the act of re-membering.

Stirring

As you continue to be present to images and memories, notice what you are feeling right now. Using your breath, create some space within you to pay attention to whatever it is that is stirring in you. If the experience feels uncomfortable, allow the breath to deepen as a way of relaxing your body into the feeling. Imagine that within you is this virgin point, this inner witness, and when you are in touch with this part of yourself you can be fully present to whatever it is you are feeling right now, but from a place of calmness, curiosity, and compassion. As you notice resistance to feelings, return to the breath again, and imagine your breath dissolving the wall within you. Remember the monastic practice of stability. See if you can stay with the stirrings of your heart and soul.

Allow as much time as you need. Continue to be aware of the images, feelings, and memories that rise up in you. You might want to continue from here to the next movement of *lectio divina*, or what you have experienced may be enough for now. Experiment with allowing this second movement to have its own time of fullness so you can explore all of its qualities and contours.

Further Possibilities for Practice

Savoring Life

Bring the practice of savoring to your everyday life by making time to savor a meal fully. Set the table with cloth napkins, plates, glasses, and silverware. As you cook, allow each act of chopping and stirring to be a prayer.

Celebrate the gift of colors, smells, and tastes. Each time you touch something, bless it in your heart, give thanks for its gift that sustains and nourishes you in the holy work of each day.

Consider also going on a slow walk through a park or a nearby garden. Allow your prayer to be a celebration of the senses and an act of gratitude for the wonders of creation. Become aware of your breath. With each inhalation, receive the smells of the earth. With each exhalation, send out love and compassion.

A participant in my workshops wrote this poem in response to her own experience of *lectio* cultivating her ability to savor life:

> This is sweet like the jars filled with raspberry
>   honey!
> This is ripe with possibility like the poppy about to
>   blossom!
> This is overflowing with the grace of transformation
>   of grief and sorrow to joy and gratitude!
> This is fragrant with the scents of new life!
> This is filled with the songs of rejoicing and grati-
>   tude! (Cathy Johnson)

Here is another description of the fruits of savoring everyday life:

> Thank you for the invitation to savor, to taste, to
> enter through "all the gates." An observation that
> I bring to the end of this week: Another sleepless
> night in a strange bed on the road where I learned
> to savor the sound of a train. What normally
> would have been an obnoxious annoyance, dis-
> turbing, ear-splitting, and interruptive, became a

lonesome wailing with a melody that riffled through the air, whose echoes beckoned me to follow them deep into the distant night.

A meditation that took a journey through a heart on fire, the discovery of a scared child who never got to be a little girl that resulted in a walk through an inferno to the other side and into an abundantly sensuous garden and a heart that can accommodate both a scared little girl and the grown-up one with at least a bit more hope of learning to trust again and the knowledge that fire sometimes devastates, sometimes transforms, and nearly always will happen again.

And finally, a new mantra, that to try to flee is madness. (Laurie Kathleen Clark)

Poetry Exploration: Cinquain

The word *cinquain* comes from *cinq*, the French word for five. Like haiku, it is a structured form that encourages the writer to express the heart of an experience in just a few words. The modern cinquain as a form of poetry is based on a word count of specific types of words. The first line is one word, which is the title of the poem, something that wants deeper exploration and expression. I suggest you begin with a word from the scriptures that has called to you. Then follow the directions for each line to see what you discover. As you write, release the thinking mind and see if you can simply allow whatever words want to come forth in response to flow out onto the page.

Line 1—One word (noun), a title or name of the subject

Line 2—Two words (adjectives) describing the title

Line 3—Three action words (verbs) ending in –ing that describe line 1. What is it doing?

Line 4—A four-word phrase or sentence that sums up or further describes line 1

Line 5—One word referring back to the title of the poem, a metaphoric synonym

For example, in response to my own prayer with the Song of Songs passage in the practice section above I wrote the following cinquain:

Delight
Sensual, succulent,
Eating, drinking, flowing,
Reveling in the senses
Holiness

Suggested Texts for *Lectio Divina*: Praying with the Senses and with Sorrow

Like cassia and camel's thorn I gave forth perfume,
and like choice myrrh I spread my fragrance,
like galbanum, onycha, and stacte,
and like the odor of incense in the tent.
Like a terebinth I spread out my branches,
and my branches are glorious and graceful.
Like the vine I bud forth delights,
and my blossoms become glorious and abundant
    fruit.

Come to me, you who desire me,
and eat your fill of my fruits.
For the memory of me is sweeter than honey,
and the possession of me sweeter than the honeycomb.
Those who eat of me will hunger for more,
and those who drink of me will thirst for more.
                    —*Ecclesiasticus 24:15–21*

How lonely sits the city
that once was full of people!
How like a widow she has become,
she that was great among the nations!
She that was a princess among the provinces
has become a vassal.

She weeps bitterly in the night,
with tears on her cheeks;
among all her lovers
she has no one to comfort her;
all her friends have dealt treacherously with her,
they have become her enemies.

Judah has gone into exile with suffering
and hard servitude;
she lives now among the nations,
and finds no resting-place;
her pursuers have all overtaken her
in the midst of her distress.

—*Lamentations 1:1–3*

But thanks be to God, who in Christ always leads us in triumphal procession, and through us spreads in every place the fragrance that comes from knowing him. For we are the aroma of Christ to God among those who are being saved and among those who are perishing; to the one a fragrance from death to death, to the other a fragrance from life to life. Who is sufficient for these things? For we are not peddlers of God's word like so many; but in Christ we speak as persons of sincerity, as persons sent from God and standing in his presence.

—*2 Corinthians 2:14–17*

I am poured out like water,
and all my bones are out of joint;
my heart is like wax;
it is melted within my breast;
my mouth is dried up like a potsherd,
and my tongue sticks to my jaws;
you lay me in the dust of death.

—*Psalm 22:14–15*

Cry aloud to the Lord! O wall of daughter Zion!
Let tears stream down like a torrent day and night!
Give yourself no rest, your eyes no respite!
Arise, cry out in the night, at the beginning of the
watches!
Pour out your heart like water before the presence
of God!

—*Lamentations 2:18–19*

You called and cried aloud and shattered my deafness.
You were radiant and resplendent, you put to flight
my blindness.
You were fragrant, and I drew in my breath and now
pant after you.
I tasted you, and I feel but hunger and thirst for you.
You touched me, and I am set on fire to attain the
peace which is yours.

—*Augustine of Hippo,* Confessions

For Reflection

What factors in your everyday life prevent you from
savoring its pleasures, such as meals, moments with
loved ones, or encounters with nature?

As children, imagination played an important role in our development as humans. Why are we often reluctant to see imagination as a beneficial tool in the development of our personal and spiritual lives as adults?

A demanding house guest, a smoker in your carpool, an office mate who doesn't recognize personal space—hospitality isn't always easy. Describe a time when you have struggled with hospitality. What feelings did you experience both emotionally and physically? What did you learn about yourself from the experience?

CHAPTER SEVEN

SUMMONING YOUR TRUE SELF

Hearing *Oratio*'s Call of the Spirit

This is the prayer of the heart on its dark journey. As the eye perceives light and the ear perceives sound, so the heart is the organ that perceives meaning. But this presupposes the courage to listen to the message and to rise to what it demands of me—the courage to say "Yes."

—David Steindl-Rast, OSB

In the previous chapter I focused on *meditatio*, the second movement of *lectio divina*, which immerses us in an experience of savoring the sacred words, listening for what they stir within us, and then making room to welcome in our feelings. In this chapter I explore the third movement, traditionally called *oratio* in Latin, which means "speech" or "address" and hence a form of prayer. Of course, all four movements of *lectio divina* are prayer; however, *oratio* refers to the kind of prayer that comes spontaneously from our hearts when we allow them to be touched by the presence of the sacred in the text. After we spend time savoring our inner experience and welcoming in our emotions, we are moved toward some kind of *response*.

In this way *oratio* encapsulates one of the overall purposes of contemplative prayer, which is to help us discern how we are to be engaged with the world. Our practice should affect our everyday lives, and *oratio* is where we listen for the specific shape of this impact. This is a subtle shift from the second movement where we tend our inner experience, to listening for the call rising out of prayer. In the third movement we discover how our experience in prayer will impact our lives. We listen for an invitation in *oratio*, a call to a new awareness and active engagement. I describe the qualities of this movement as summoning and serving. Thus, *oratio* is about hearing the call of the Spirit and responding.

Ultimately, we claim our deepest gifts in service to others. This chapter will explore the movement of call and response, and connect it to the practices of humility, compunction of the heart, and discernment.

HUMILITY, TRUTH-TELLING, AND SELF-CARE

At the root of humility is the Greek word *humus*, which means "earth" or "earthiness"—the earth that God made and called good, the earth from which God fashioned us. Humility is the fundamental recognition that we each draw our life and breath from the same source—the God who made us and calls us beloved. Humility prevents us from seeing ourselves as more deserving or graced than another person. It also compels us to recognize that we are no less deserving or graced than another. Humility draws us into mutual relation, through which we allow no abuse, no demeaning, no diminishment of others or of ourselves. Through humility we can let go of the quest for perfection. "When it comes to living together," Roberta Bondi writes in her book *To Pray and to Love*, "humility is the opposite of perfectionism. It gives up unrealistic expectations of how things ought to be for a clear vision of what human life is really like. In turn, this enables its possessors to see and thus love the people they deeply desire to love."[1]

Humility also calls us to recognize our radical dependence on the One who created us as well as our kinship with those who share the earth with us. Benedict's longest chapter in the Rule, Chapter Seven, is on the topic of humility—a virtue he saw as essential to monastic life. He describes twelve steps toward cultivating the virtue of humility. The desert is a place that teaches us this kind of radical humility: "In the desert it is impossible to forget who and what we are. Our fragility brings us back to the Living One, 'in whom we live and move and have our being.' We discover again our essential axis…. The memory of the Living One quickens life within us. It centers us on the contemplation of the One who is at the heart of who we are."[2] I love this image of "our essential axis."

Humility means remembering our human limitations. It is about learning that saying no is equally as important as saying yes. In the third movement of *oratio*, furthermore, we are listening for an invitation or call, although it doesn't always mean we listen for something more to add to our already full plates. Identifying what we are *not* called to do is essential to discovering what we are being summoned to do. Sometimes *oratio* will lead us to simplify our lives, to let go of what is no longer necessary or what distracts us from our heart's deep desires. After all, we live in a world with so many good and worthy opportunities in which to invest our precious energy that we can feel pulled in many directions. Humility reminds us that we are not asked to be all things to all people, but to nurture our unique gifts and to recognize that self-care is good stewardship of those gifts. Humility demands truth-telling and radical self-honesty; it is about celebrating the gifts we have been uniquely given in service of others, as well as recognizing our limitations and vulnerability.

We can bring humility to the practice of *lectio divina* in a number of ways. Humility is intertwined with the commitment to conversion that we reflected on in Chapter Three: to recognize that we are always growing, that we never know the fullness of the Divine Spirit, and so we will allow the text to surprise us with its insight for our lives. Humility is also deeply connected to the practice of simplicity we explored in Chapter Five, and the call to let go of those things that no longer serve us. When we practice humility with the sacred text we also release our expectations and judgments, and embrace the limitations of our own understanding. We surrender our desire for perfection in our prayer—whether that means giving up on getting the steps exactly right or giving up on trying to achieve an unrealistic ideal. Many of the participants in my retreats and workshops discover a profound sense of freedom when they realize that the effort to get the prayer "just right" was interfering with their intimacy and encounter with God. Having a "perfect" prayer experience became the goal rather than resting in God's presence. One woman later told me that she recognized this was her key issue in all of life, but acknowledging it in *lectio divina* first helped free her from the demands she made on herself all the time. She was freed to seek God in each moment rather than realizing some preconceived ideal of what she should be doing with her life.

Humility can also help us be present to the challenge of engaging difficult biblical texts and what they might have to teach us. In the introduction to *A Guide to Living the Truth*, a book that focuses on humility, Benedictine scholar and monk Michael Casey offers a keen reminder that "a much more creative way of dealing with difficult texts is to take our negative reaction as an indication that there may be an issue beneath the surface with which we must deal."[3] Similar to what we explored in the previous chapter—paying attention to our energetic response to a text—those places in our reading that make us squirm, or the ideas with which we wrestle, are often the ones that bear the greatest fruit in terms of revealing our own hidden places of resistance and fear.

Humility means setting aside the mask, a kind of nakedness where we allow ourselves to be seen without social convention, presenting ourselves in all of our vulnerability. Orthodox theologian Jean-Yves Leloup summarizes it this way:

> The great secret of interior peace is humility. It is well known that one of the sources of anguish and anxiety is to test the difference between who one pretends to be and who one really is. To be as you are, adding nothing, taking nothing away, pretending no longer, accepting your earthiness, strengths and weaknesses.[4]

Ultimately, humility arises from a softened heart, one that has released it armor and defensiveness and is open to the surprising ways of God. This is also one of the goals of *lectio*. Honoring our limits as creatures can be deeply liberating. We must have patience with the unfolding of our lives and the world. God's kingdom unfolds in God's own time. We discover that we are not solely responsible for saving the world. Acknowledging our limits can liberate us from our compulsions and frantic busyness and lead us toward recognizing our interdependence. Humility is a foundational place from which to begin discernment. It is there that we temper our tendency to become overwhelmed by the pressing needs of the world's problems.

COMPUNCTION: AWAKENING YOUR AUTHENTIC SELF

> *Native Americans describe spirituality as having a*
> *"moist heart," perhaps because native wisdom knows*
> *the soil of the human heart is necessarily watered*
> *with tears; and that tears keep the ground soft. From*
> *such ground new life is born.*
> —*Maria Harris*, Dance of the Spirit

Compunction means the pricking or stimulation of the heart. In monastic tradition, compunction is often referred to as arising from our encounters with the sacred texts. In *Sacred Reading*, Michael Casey describes compunction as "the word of God awaken[ing] in us our latent spiritual sense; we become aware of realities that, until this, had been forced below the threshold of our minds: God's call, our need for God, our desire to have a different kind of life."[5] Compunction stirs feelings like those in *meditatio*, but in *oratio* they are the result of a deepened awareness of who we are called to be. Often when we touch this place inside us, we experience the sorrow of having been blind to it for so long. Casey goes on to write:

> *Lectio divina* is not only a means of discovering something about God; it also helps to understand our hidden selves. It is not the alienating absorption of a message that is foreign or even hostile to our own deepest aspirations; it is the surprising conclusion that our most authentic level of being is mirrored in the Scriptures.[6]

In *meditatio*, the second movement, we explored making space for the feelings that are stirred within us in response to our encounter with the sacred text. In the transition into the third movement, which can be very subtle, these feelings deepen in us. We begin to listen to their meaning for us, and what they are calling us to do in our lives. There are a number of ways compunction can manifest itself in the heart. When we become present to our emotional landscape and the way our heart is stirring in response to the words we have heard, we can come to deeper insights about who we are called to be and what we are called to do. When we engage at this deep soul level we will experience not only joy but also sorrow. Joy arrives with a deeper understanding of who we truly are; sorrow arises when we grieve over how long we have lived in inauthentic ways.

These feelings don't always accompany each prayer experience, but over time they are an integral part of our *lectio divina* practice. Compunction comes through both the grace of God as well as our own openheartedness. As with our practice in *meditatio*, in *oratio* we continue to make space to welcome in our experience and feelings, but we are moved to an even deeper level where these feelings begin to transform us into more compassionate persons. Instead of reading for information, when we practice *lectio divina* we read to be changed, transformed into a more authentic expression of ourselves and who God molded us to be at the very instant of our creation. We allow God to do this work not just through ideas but also through the world of our emotions.

We may be surprised to discover a great sadness we cannot name and whose roots we cannot identify. Or perhaps we may suddenly recognize all the ways we have been distracting ourselves from what is most important. Or we have an insight that may change our attitudes or how we act. This is the moment when we move into the third stage of *lectio divina*. It is often the result of a back-and-forth process between the second and third movements, a spiraling between savoring and stirring and then attending to how we are being summoned from this experience. Remember that the path of *lectio divina* is not meant to be linear, and the boundaries between movements are not solid.

There is a longstanding tradition within Christian practice of honoring the gift of tears. John Chryssavgis writes in *Into the Heart of the Desert: The Spirituality of the Desert Fathers and Mothers*: "Tears and weeping indicate a significant frontier in the way of the desert. They bespeak a promise. In fact, they are the only way into the heart."[7] This frontier is the boundary between our old way of seeing and believing and the wide new expansiveness into which praying with Scripture calls us. In his rule, Benedict describes these as tears of compunction and prayer with tears. Compunction awakens us to all the ways we have been false to our own deepest self and to the profound longing that is kindled when we pay attention to the heart. Allowing your own tears to flow is part of the prayer experience. Your inner witness can behold this expression of tenderness with compassion for yourself.

DISCERNMENT: VALUING THE VOICES OF DIFFERENCE

Only with awakened hearts are we actually able to ful-
fill our purpose within the cosmos and take our place
in that great dance of divine manifestation.
—*Cynthia Bourgeault*, The Wisdom
Way of Knowing

If the third movement of *lectio divina* is about listening for the call to my life right now, then humility helps me stay grounded in this process and recognize both my gifts and my limitations. The summons spoken in this moment of the prayer experience will often touch on both of these—it calls us to release whatever gets in the way of our service and to live more deeply into our giftedness, to find ways to share our gifts more freely and widely with others. Tears of compunction can help me recognize that something important has been touched within me.

We engage the tools of discernment when we are hoping to make a change in our lives or are listening for a new direction. The practice of discernment is listening for the ways we are being called to live our lives by God and learning to discriminate between the multitude of voices and messages in our lives. The Christian scriptures' Greek word *diakrisis*, meaning "discerning," "judging," or "distinguishing," appears in 1 Corinthians 12:10, where Paul describes the different spiritual gifts and includes among them the "discernment of spirits." In the letter to the Hebrews, discernment is described as the gift of maturity, possessed by "those whose faculties have been trained by practice to distinguish good from evil" (5:14). At a later time the desert mothers and fathers described *diakrisis* as central to the way of life for the monk. Discernment is a way of being in the world where we listen daily for God's subtle call to us to open our hearts in new ways. As I come to know God more intimately through the sacred texts, this deepening wisdom of the heart leads me to more easily discern God's desires for me in all areas of my life. Discernment impacts my friendships, my work, my relationship to my body, and my sense of responsibility for the flourishing of nature.

Discernment, moreover, is a gift of the spirit and calls us to notice the sources of our thoughts, whether from God or from other voices in our lives. We listen and try to distinguish between them. The first two movements have prepared us for this process: we have centered ourselves and moved into a heart-centered space, paid attention to the word or phrase that is called to us, and given space to savor and notice what is stirring in us through image, feeling, and memory. All three of these faculties play a role in the practice of discernment. A wise discernment process must emerge from the heart, which is the place of integration. The heart is where our thoughts, emotions, imagination, and intuition come together. In our time of savoring we have been cultivating our ability to ponder in new ways by opening ourselves to playful associations and exploring new metaphors and symbols. By tending to our feelings in *oratio*, we discover the ways we have opened or closed ourselves to God.

We find some profound wisdom for discernment in the Rule of Benedict with regard to the necessity to include a diversity of voices:

> Whenever any important business has to be done in the monastery, let the Abbot call together the whole community and state the matter to be acted upon. Then, having heard the brethren's advice, let him turn the matter over

in his own mind and do what he shall judge to be most expedient. The reason we have said that all should be called for counsel is that the Lord often reveals to the younger what is best.[8]

This regard for diversity is connected to the monastic practice of hospitality, where all are welcomed in as the presence of the Sacred, especially the stranger. We explored this in *meditatio* with regard to welcoming in our emotions. In our *lectio divina* practice, we welcome in the stranger in other ways, too. In prayer we are called upon to listen attentively to those parts of ourselves we might assume to have nothing important to say, or to reflect on the people in our lives who offer us wisdom we might want to reject before even considering it. The process Benedict desribes values the voices of difference and allows time to hear their stories. In order for the discernment process to fruitfully serve the search for truth, it must be marked not by exclusion but by hospitality and inclusion.

THE MANY PATHS OF RESPONSE

> *Vocation is fundamentally a call to relationship....*
> *A voice not our own calls to us daily with invitation.*
> *A power from beyond ourselves sends forth a word to*
> *evoke a response of shared power.*
> —*Norvene Vest*, Friend of the Soul

Oratio draws on the practice of simplicity, addressing the question, How am I to free my heart to respond in service and compassion? For this reason, we are called to release our tight grip on what we think the text is saying to us and listen to the possibilities that emerge simply from allowing time to be in relationship with the text through mind, heart, imagination, and memory. We release our own assumptions, expectations, and judgments.

We bring this openness at the start of our prayer, but each movement of *lectio divina* calls us to commit again and again to this radical posture of openness. If we are truly open, we will encounter possible ways of responding that we might not otherwise have considered. As Esther de Waal writes of careful listening,

> To listen attentively to what we hear is much more than giving it passing aural attention. It means in the first instance we have to listen whether we like it or not, whether we hear what we want to or something that is disagreeable or threatening…. If we stop listening to what we find hard to take then, as the Abbot of St Benoit-sur-Loire puts it in a striking phrase, "We're likely to pass God by without even noticing him."[9]

Retreat participant Roxanne Morgan describes her experience of increased attentiveness with *lectio divina* in a similar way: "This is what spoke to me today, went with me throughout today—'The earth is full of the steadfast love of the Lord.' The past few days have been full of caring for my folks, schooling my youngest, laundry, liturgy, quotidien mysteries … these words have been an anchor for me, making me look closer and *truly see* what is before me." Her response to prayer was to bring deeper attention to everything she already does.

Discernment, however, does not always lead us to act out of complete certainty. Part of the call of a discerning way of life is to rest in questions and the tensions of life without always trying to resolve them. *Meditatio*, the second movement of *lectio divina*, with its emphasis on making space for images and feelings, gives us access to those dimensions of ourselves that cultivate our capacity to rest in "both/and" rather than "either/or." Sometimes we are simply called to act upon the call we hear and in our response we discover new layers of the discernment. Sometimes we can become paralyzed by the idea of trying to figure out exactly God's will, as if God has only one option available to us and gives us the burden of trying to figure out what it is.

Instead, I prefer to imagine a much more expansive and spacious God, one who offers life-giving paths out of a variety of directions we might choose. Often discernment is a choice between many goods. Spiritual maturity comes with making enough space to listen but then taking responsibility for our actions and living into them, knowing that we are always on the path without ever fully knowing its potential. Often we have to say no to very good and appealing possibilities in order to move forward in one direction. If discernment is a way of life, as is *lectio divina*, then the two enter into a life-giving dance where we continue throughout our lives to listen for ways to respond wholeheartedly.

Judy Smoot, a fellow Benedictine oblate, offers this story of how *lectio divina* supported her in saying no:

> I carved out this time for *lectio divina* first thing in the morning and am so glad that I did. I was captured by the phrase "Go out in joy and be led back in peace" (Isaiah 55:12). I was then struck by "Bring forth and sprout" (Isaiah 55:10) as a companion piece. As I moved into my day it seemed what I most want to recall is that when I go out, when I serve with joy, peace comes to me. I am aware of the times I serve not from a place of joy and become depleted and can push against the very things that I most love to be about. Very little that is healthy sprouts when I serve from that place.
>
> I work with a group of women who provide a listening circle for homeless women in a variety of venues—a women's shelter, family shelter, and transitional housing. It has been hard for me to hang on to this commitment given an increasingly full schedule. I was at the ministry's companion's meeting this morning and there was conversation

about additional ministry needs that have become hard to fill at some of the shelters. I so wanted to say yes to more, but held on to my sacred no. I did, however, offer to do one small thing that was within my capacity. It ended up being a very huge thing that has likely resulted in another volunteer coming on board. I did what I could do with joy, was given peace, and a seed sprouted as a result.

On a similar note, Norvene Vest writes in *Gathered in the Word*: "*Lectio* intends that we bring to bear in word/activity those inner certainties experienced in silence/rest. In *lectio*, we seek to experience rest in order to let it inform our daily struggles, decisions, and actions."[10] Whatever is happening within your heart, God is active in bringing forth growth so that it bears fruit in the world.

In *lectio divina*, however, we are not always looking for something else to add to our growing "to do" list, but to discover more and more ways to infuse love into all of our actions and encounter the deep Self and its unique way of being in the world. After praying *lectio divina* with Isaiah 50:4–5, one teacher wrote this poem about her experience of being summoned to take herself and her vocation more seriously:

> Do I possess
> The tongue of a teacher?
>
> One who feeds others
> with a word
> with open ears
> and an open heart?
>
> Do not turn away
> this is your life
> your sacred word
> your sacred work. (Deb Swingholm)

Invitation to Practice: Summoning and Serving

In this practice I invite you to focus more of your time and energy in prayer on the third movement of summoning and serving. What follows is a way of moving into the experience. Listen to how you are being led to continue the prayer.

Consider beginning your prayer with the first few verses of Psalm 139:

> O LORD, you have searched me and known me.
> You know when I sit down and when I rise up;
> you discern my thoughts from far away.
> You search out my path and my lying down,
> and are acquainted with all my ways.

Settling and Shimmering

Begin your practice by settling into your body and paying attention to your breath. Allow the rhythm of your breathing to slow you down and settle you in this moment and place. Gently draw your awareness from your head down into your heart. Take as much time as you need to feel present.

Now read the text through once or twice, and listen for a word or phrase that is calling to you today. Notice what is shimmering in the midst of the sacred text, inviting your loving prayer.

Savoring and Stirring

Savor this word or phrase and sink into an experience of it. Begin to allow your imagination to unfold and bloom wide. Be aware of the images and memories moving in you.

Witness the feelings that rise up. Welcome in the experience you are having, keeping a connection to your breath as a centering place and way to continue paying attention to what is moving through you.

Summoning

The movement from the second to third phase of *lectio divina* can be subtle. Sometimes you might intentionally shift your attention to listen for the call bubbling up in your prayer. But you might also discover that as you welcome in the full spectrum of your feelings, you have an experience of compunction arising in your heart. Perhaps you notice an upwelling of deep joy and sense of God's overflowing abundance in your life, or sense that the word shimmering is in alignment with a new path you have been considering for your life. Or you might notice a sense of sadness, an ache in your heart as if you have been pierced. You might also experience deep grief as you come to recognize how you have resisted God's call until now, how you have set up all kinds of distractions in your life, and suddenly you become aware that your life will one day end and you will not have embraced it fully.

You may also experience a sense of being pulled or drawn forward into a new way of understanding or into a new action. You may experience God luring you into a recognition of your own deep desires. Place your hand over your heart and see whether making a physical connection helps ground this experience in your body.

Serving

As you continue to listen, is there a sense of invitation emerging? This may not be a grand and life-changing call; more often it is a subtle movement toward something that is more life-giving than life-changing. Perhaps it is a summons to let go of old patterns of thinking that are holding you back from living your life more fully, or a desire to extend yourself in reconciliation with a friend with whom you have had a misunderstanding.

Lectio divina can cultivate in us a heart of greater peace over time, but the movement of the prayer is always from our inner world to the outer world. We are called to consider how our prayer practice is changing our habitual ways of being or drawing us into a new sense of purpose. Our prayer is meant to be enfleshed, embodied in our daily lives. The practice of *lectio divina* demands a gradual softening of our hearts and opening in compassion to ourselves, others, and all of creation.

Take as much time as you need to tend to this sense of invitation growing in you. Then allow yourself a few moments of stillness, releasing the thoughts and ideas moving through your mind, and come to rest in your heart in the presence of God.

Further Possibilities for Practice

Finding a Soul Friend

The inner movements of our prayer can be very powerful, and sometimes it is difficult to distinguish the voices speaking with us because our own inner judgments can be so loud. Or perhaps we hear God's call to a radically new direction but are uncertain whether our hesitancy to respond is because of fear and resistance or because we are not entirely sure whether we are really hearing the Divine Voice.

We don't have to take this journey alone. When we listen to these voices, it can be confusing at times, which is why being immersed in a community and meeting regularly with a soul friend or spiritual companion can be invaluable. In the desert tradition, people were encouraged to share their discernment with a wise elder. We also benefit from testing out the fruits of our prayer. When we find ourselves growing more in our ability to have compassion for ourselves and others, we can be certain that the Spirit is at work. However, sometimes we may find our own motivations getting in the way, such as our desire for a certain kind of affirmation from others, or for a specific kind of success and achievement.

Choose one person in your life with whom to share the fruits and insights of prayer, who will also help ground you in the wider context of a community and a tradition. This person should be someone who knows you well and who can help you test out your discernment to see whether it is emerging from the deep heart and authentic self. In Chapter Four I discuss further the role a good spiritual director can play in the journey of deepening prayer.

Poetry Exploration: The Acrostic Poem

An acrostic poem is one in which the first letter of each line spells out a word. In the Hebrew scriptures, the Lamentations of Jeremiah as well as some of the proverbs and psalms are written as acrostics of the Hebrew alphabet.

Consider taking the word or phrase from your prayer experience and writing it vertically down the page. Then allow the letters to be the prompt for the line of poetry that follows. You might consider allowing the poem to express the essence of the invitation that has risen out of the text, or else let it be part of a process of discovery, seeing what each line wants to say as you come to it. Writing poetry from a heart-centered place and releasing our thinking and judging mind can lead us to new places and images.

Below are some examples of acrostic poems written by workshop participants in response to their *lectio divina* experience:

You Hem Me In
Yahweh,
Open my heart
Unlock my mind

Have mercy on me!
Embrace
Me with your LOVE and compassion
Make me whole again
Enter my life fully
Inner to outer
Newness (Eileen Downard)

Search
Seeking you out
Everywhere, but the simplest place to find you
Alone in my heart.
Return to this moment and
Contemplate the words written.
How simple it really is. (Eveline Maedel)

Path
Present
Awake
To
Hope (Roxanne Morgan)

Suggested Text for *Lectio Continua*: Invitation

In this chapter I suggest you try an experience of *lectio continua*, which means to pray over several days with a continuous text. As described in an earlier chapter, the ancient monks would often choose a book of the Bible and then pray their way slowly through it, stopping each time a word or phrase called their attention. At the beginning of this practice section you had the first three verses of Psalm 139, a text about the God who knows us and our call in life more intimately than we know ourselves. Now try praying with a longer version of the psalm in order to experience *lectio continua*.

O LORD, you have searched me and known me.
You know when I sit down and when I rise up;
you discern my thoughts from far away.
You search out my path and my lying down,
and are acquainted with all my ways.
Even before a word is on my tongue,
O LORD, you know it completely.
You hem me in, behind and before,
and lay your hand upon me.
Such knowledge is too wonderful for me;
it is so high that I cannot attain it.

Where can I go from your spirit?
Or where can I flee from your presence?
If I ascend to heaven, you are there;
if I make my bed in Sheol, you are there.
If I take the wings of the morning
and settle at the farthest limits of the sea,
even there your hand shall lead me,
and your right hand shall hold me fast.
If I say, "Surely the darkness shall cover me,
and the light around me become night,"
even the darkness is not dark to you;
the night is as bright as the day,
for darkness is as light to you.

For it was you who formed my inward parts;
you knit me together in my mother's womb.
I praise you, for I am fearfully and wonderfully
    made.
Wonderful are your works;
that I know very well.
My frame was not hidden from you,
when I was being made in secret,
intricately woven in the depths of the earth.

Your eyes beheld my unformed substance.
In your book were written
all the days that were formed for me,
when none of them as yet existed.
How weighty to me are your thoughts, O God!
How vast is the sum of them!
I try to count them—they are more than the sand;
I come to the end—I am still with you.

—*Psalm 139:1–18*

For Reflection

Describe a time that you acted "out of character." At what point did you realize that your response was not authentically you? What were the driving factors that caused you to act the way you did?

In what ways have you been tempted to pursue perfection?

Describe a time when you acknowledged your limits to another person by saying no. What emotions did this stir in you? What reaction did you receive from the other person?

What are the most important qualities for your soul friend or spiritual companion to have?

CHAPTER EIGHT

THE GIFT OF BEING

Resting in *Contemplatio*'s Stillness and Silence

*Silence is the home of the word. Silence gives
strength and fruitfulness to the word. We can even
say that words are meant to disclose the mystery of
the silence from which they come.*
           Henri Nouwen, The Way of the Heart

The fourth movement of *lectio* is called *contemplatio*, which is Latin for "contemplation." While the whole process of *lectio divina* is considered contemplative prayer, *contemplatio* is the culmination of the previous three movements and the time when we enter more deeply into a state of being with God. In *contemplatio* the invitation is to slow ourselves down even further, release all the words, thoughts, images, memories, and invitations that have emerged in our prayer, and rest even more deeply into the presence of God, simply relishing the gift of being. In contemplation we surrender ourselves into the presence of the One who is the source of all. The stillness of heart to which we are called in contemplative prayer is not a void or an absence of sound, but a rich and vibrant presence.

Following the third movement, where we listen for the call and discern how we are moved to respond, the fourth movement offers us a counterbalance to this experience. We are called in this time to remember who we are without focusing on what we are to do. *Contemplatio* calls us to release our doing; the more we strive for this state of being, the more our energy is focused on the work of achieving a particular experience. Contemplative prayer means a simultaneous alertness and opening, while also releasing our desire to feel a specific way and simply receive the prayer as gift.

KATAPHATIC AND APOPHATIC PRAYER

In Christian spirituality there have traditionally been two ways of encountering God. The first is through what is known as *kataphatic* prayer, or the path of images, where words, symbols, images, and ideas all come into play. The first three movements of *lectio* follow this way of coming to know God. We listen for the words shimmering, the feelings and images stirring, the sense of invitation summoning us in this moment of our lives. We savor our experience through all of our senses, relishing the way we come to know the Holy through taste, touch, smell, sound, and sight. In *kataphatic* prayer we tend to express our understanding of God through metaphor. For example, Psalm 18:2 describes God as a rock, while Psalm 23:1 sees God as a shepherd and Psalm 27:1 invokes God as light. Jesus' parables are filled with images meant to evoke new understandings of God and what God's reign looks like in our midst. In Matthew 13 we have the largest collection of these "kingdom" parables, where the kingdom of heaven is compared to a tiny mustard seed that grows into a large tree (verse 32), a measure of yeast in flour (verse 33), and a hidden treasure in a field (verses 44–46). All this imagery would have given Jesus' followers new and surprising insights into God and God's ways. This way of prayer is also characteristic of the spiritual exercises of Ignatius of Loyola, discussed earlier, which rely on the use of imagination in prayer, particularly imaginings of the life of Jesus portrayed in the gospels.

At some point in our experience of prayer, however, we need to recognize that while we develop our relationship with God through image and sense experience, God is ultimately beyond all these ways of perceiving, even beyond human understanding itself. At some point we need to release our images and ideas of God because they will always fall short of the infinite and expansive reality from which the universe emerged. As soon as we create an image, we also create a framework and a limitation. As soon as we begin to cling to an image of God as a rock or a shepherd, it becomes difficult to imagine the Divine in any other way.

There is a complementary path to the *kataphatic* way, however, which is known as the *apophatic* way, or "the path of unknowing." It is wordless and free of all content, including symbols, images, and thoughts. This way of darkness means entering the profound mystery of God and allowing ourselves to move beyond images and dualities. When we enter the *apophatic* way, we are called to enter into paradox. We no longer have to reconcile opposites. We recognize how little we know of God, so we can't say God is this way or that way; God is *both* and *neither*. This path requires a radical sense of humility and embrace of our limited vision. God is beyond our ability to understand or grasp.

THE CLOUD OF UNKNOWING AND CENTERING PRAYER

There is a rich history in Christian tradition of the *apophatic* way of prayer. Perhaps best known is a fourteenth-century work called *The Cloud of Unknowing* by an anonymous author who describes the practice of contemplative prayer. The book counsels that we seek God not through thoughts but through love. The use of our intellect is by stages stripped away until only love remains. For the author of the *Cloud*, contemplation is a spiritual union with God through the heart.

In contemporary times there has been a reclaiming of the gifts of Christian contemplative prayer, especially through the method of "centering prayer" by Trappist monks William Menninger,

Thomas Keating, and Basil Pennington. They created a system of prayer rooted in ancient practices such as *lectio divina*, and the writings of great mystics like John Cassian, Teresa of Avila, John of the Cross, Therese of Lisieux, and Thomas Merton as well as the author of *The Cloud of Unknowing*. This practice became known as centering prayer because of Thomas Merton's description of contemplative prayer as prayer "centered entirely on the presence of God." Using this method, we choose a sacred word as our anchor and allow it to draw us more deeply into an awareness of God's presence. Each time we become distracted we gently return to the sacred word.

When we embrace this aspect of prayer, we move into an experience of having our deepest convictions shaken and our reliable frameworks wrested from our grasp. Most of us live under the illusion that we have ultimate control over our lives, and that is why it often takes an experience of profound loss and grief to enter into the *apophatic* way of prayer. Intellectually, we may understand that God is far beyond any image we can create, but to experience in the depth of our being the "great unknowing" of God can be a truly terrifying experience. The *apophatic* way is the slow work of deconstructing our most beloved ideas and idols, leading us into a naked experience of the Real. The mystics describe this stage of prayer as a purification process, although in the midst of it we may feel utterly abandoned or without hope. That is why it is usually best to embark on this form of prayer with a trusted spiritual director or teacher.

When my mother died, I was bereft, and all the ways I had imagined God's presence in my life suddenly felt void of meaning or truth. I entered a long period of darkness, which I later came to understand as a journey into unknowing. The theology that had sustained me for many years could not withstand this kind of loss and heartbreak, but before I could mature into a new way of encountering God I had to be stripped of the old.

Inner Noise, Stilling, and Equanimity

> One of the great paradoxes of the spiritual life is that
> our struggles are not separate from the luminous
> vastness within each of us. We don't get rid of strug-
> gle to discover this open space; nor does its discovery
> necessarily rid us of our struggles. The riddle of the
> obstacle is solved not by pushing it away or by hold-
> ing on to it, but by meeting it with silence and by
> discovering in this meeting that sacred ground,
> which upholds both joy and sorrow, both struggle
> and freedom from struggle. When we realize this we
> will struggle less with our struggles and we will
> have solved by our own silence the riddles that guard
> the doorway into the silent land.
> —Martin Laird, Into the Silent Land

Our world is filled with outer noise: traffic, television, radio,
phones ringing or e-mail notifications dinging, our friends and
family chattering away, the dog barking. The practice of stillness
is in part to seek out ways to cultivate silence around us. This is
the appeal of going away on retreat—we enter into an environment that offers in the outer world a reflection of what we are
seeking within.

The heart of the contemplative journey is the movement
toward inner stillness. When we first enter into a place of complete outer stillness, we will find that our minds are clamoring
with thoughts and voices vying for our attention. Sometimes this
is enough to make us avoid silence altogether. Indeed, I suspect
that is part of the drive behind the constant noise we fill our lives
with. With this constant chorus and cacophony, we can avoid the
hard work of listening to the noise that fills our hearts.

When we first begin to practice any kind of contemplative
prayer, it is normal to experience a heightened awareness of inner

voices, constant commentary, judgments, and chatter within. Throughout our lives we will wrestle with these to varying degrees. It is part of our human nature to have active minds.

What the practice of contemplative prayer offers us is an arena in which we can cultivate the ability to become present to this internal noise—acknowledging it and letting it go. Sometimes the work is to notice the specific thoughts and become curious about them, uncovering the hidden narrative that drives our lives and compulsions. For example, I wrestle with perfectionism, facing an exhausting chorus of voices that is never satisfied with any effort I make because, of course, perfection is unattainable. In contemplative prayer I can become conscious of these thoughts and actively release them when they rise up, rather than allowing them to distract me from the goal of my prayer, which is being in the presence of God. If I think that I will never pray well enough or write well enough, I am far less likely to even try. Through my prayer practice, I notice when my inner chorus of critical voices begins before I get too far down the road of inner judgment and negativity. I recognize these judgments for what they are—illusions that keep me from growing in my intimacy with God.

The ancient desert monks wrote extensively about the kinds of thoughts we are likely to encounter in the stillness of prayer. From anger to laziness to lustfulness, these thoughts were met and named for what they are—perversions of ourselves, distractions from the movement toward our deepest, most authentic self. How they worked with these was to cultivate their opposites, the virtues. When we find ourselves impatient, we seek to bring the quality of patience to our lives; when we find ourselves angry or resentful, we seek to bring gratitude. The work is to first notice the thoughts rising and meet them with compassion and curiosity. If our mind is racing or we feel filled with anxiety or uneasiness, we return to the breath as a way of calming both body and mind. We then seek to cultivate the virtue in our hearts that helps us quell the insistence of this voice within us. We slowly move to the place of releasing thoughts altogether, where we can forget our small selves and open ourselves to the Holy Other in which we find rest.

In Chapter Six we explored the role of the inner witness and the virgin point of the soul as that calm, curious, and compassionate place in ourselves. When grief arises, the inner witness helps us recognize it as an energy that is not the sum total of who we are, but part of our experience in that moment. We can breathe and allow the energy of grief to move through us rather than resisting it. We still feel the pain, but because we are not fighting against it, our grief does not get stuck and amplified in the body. This is how we cultivate our ability to connect to this calm, non-anxious presence to whatever we are experiencing. When we practice and cultivate this in prayer, we slowly discover how to bring this inner quiet to more and more aspects of our lives.

As we grow in inner stillness, we move toward true silence. Stillness is a quality necessary to experience the depth of silence. They are intimately linked. Once we move inward and clear away the inner dialogue, we can discover the kind of silence that is not just the absence of noise, but the profound presence of God. As Thomas Keating says, "God's first language is silence. Everything else is a translation."

SILENCE IN CONTEMPLATIVE PRAYER

> *I stand at the threshold and wait. Watching, listening, scanning the horizon. My soul is filled with wonder and beauty. My lungs expand with deep breathing from the beginning of time. Silence fills my breath, penetrating deep into my core and the outer reaches of my toes, fingers and very tips of the ends of the hairs on my head. I am filled: with breath, silence, beauty, wonder, hope, vastness and*

expanse. Deep blue skies, puffy clouds, green grass
and carpets of wildflowers.... I cross the threshold
and enter in. (Sharon Richards)

What is spiritual silence? It is not just the absence of talk. Silence has substance. It is the presence of something. Thomas Merton claims that silence is our admission that we have broken communication with God and are now willing to listen. We can be reduced to silence in times of doubt, uncertainty, nothingness, and awe. When we have exhausted all our human efforts, experienced the limitations of human justice, or known the finitude of human relationships, we are left with silence. Those who have experienced the sacrament of failure are more likely to know the emptying power of silence, as Martin Laird writes in his book on silence and contemplation:

> The practice of silence nourishes vigilance, self-knowledge, letting go, and the compassionate embrace of all whom we would otherwise be quick to condemn. Gradually we realize that whatever it is in us that sees the mind games we play is itself free of all such mind games and is utterly silence, pure, vast, and free. When we realize we are the *awareness* and not the drama unfolding in our awareness our lives are freer, simpler, more compassionate. Fear remains frightening but we are not afraid of fear. Pain still hurts, but we are not hurt by pain.[1]

Like *Shavasana* ("corpse pose") for relaxation at the end of yoga practice, the entry into and embrace of silence is in the service of our own growing wholeness. According to an Islamic proverb, "If speech is silver, silence is gold." In the teachings of the Buddha, there is a close link between truth and silence:

Satya, the word translated "truth" in English, is one of the oldest words in the Indian religious heritage. It too has a wealth of meanings. Derived from the root *sat*, meaning "being," "existence," "pure," "holy," "perfect," etc., *satya* signifies the Truth in all its unlimited perfection and plenitude. As the ground of all existence, *satya* can only be experienced through the medium of Silence. It cannot be expressed. The moment one tries to express it, one runs the danger of falsifying it, of rendering it *asatya*, "untruth." The fountain of Silence is the sole medium that is capable of delivering the Truth.[2]

The silence of the Buddha is not simply an absence of words or noise, but possesses a transforming power, bringing us closer to the truth of things. As Benedict wrote in his rule, "Monks should diligently cultivate silence at all times, but especially at night" (42:1). Night is the great teacher of the source of all silence. It is at night that we can discover the immense stillness at the heart of everything.

The Orthodox tradition has a powerful tradition of silence that, together with the desert mothers and fathers, forms the foundation of much of the Christian mystical relationship to silence. Metropolitan Kallistos of Diokleia writes that to reach a state of silence is one of the most challenging things we do in prayer: "Silence is not merely negative—a pause between words, a temporary cessation of speech—but, properly understood, it is highly positive: an attitude of attentive alertness, of vigilance, and above all of listening."[3] When we listen with this kind of attention we listen to the prayer of our own heart and understand that it is the voice of another speaking within us.

If the *kataphatic* way celebrates God's intimate nearness and incarnate presence in everything, then the *apophatic* way confronts us with God's radical transcendence that neither our minds nor our senses can ever grasp. Only silence comes close to allowing us to experience what this divine Otherness means. We have to admit all the ways we co-opt the idea of God for our own purposes, both individually and in community. Daily we hear people utter all kinds of certainties about who God is, often at the expense of the freedom and dignity of others. When we enter into the profound experience of *unknowing*, however, we speak with much more humility about what we do and do not know about God's nature. This path of unknowing is an antidote to the literalism and fundamentalism so rampant in our world. But because it is not an easy path, one that requires us to release our illusions of control and our idols of God, most of us do not even embark on the journey until life events confront us with this truth.

Silence also has an integrative function. *Lectio divina* can stir up a great many images and symbols that speak to the new reality being birthed within us. In this fourth movement we recognize the need to step back and simply be with what is happening in us, allowing it to ripen slowly without our being actively involved. We enter the wisdom of night, the place where we can honor that which is nameless within us, that which is still seed and not blossom. We release all of our thoughts, desires, and strivings, and simply rest in the presence of the One Who Is, already there with us in the sacred space of our hearts.

Cultivating Contentment

> *The still heart that refuses nothing.*
> —Jane Hirshfield, "Lake and Maple"

The Rule of Benedict counsels contentment, which essentially means being fully satisfied with whatever is being presented to us in a given moment. It is the satisfaction of desire. Being content often means shifting what it is we desire so that we can grow more satisfied with what we already have. Benedict wanted us to remember that every gift and grace we have comes from God, and to marvel that there is something rather than nothing. We won't grow spiritually if we are always striving after something bigger and better, for maturity comes from cultivating a sense of contentment with the lives we already have.

I learned a great deal about contentment from my yoga practice. In Sanskrit the word for contentment is *santosha*, which asks us to accept the current state as it truly is, and work with the resources we have available to us rather than forcing or pushing to achieve the goals of our egos. Contentment calls for a release of our resistance to what life brings us. It can be a very subtle opening. I had practiced an openhearted welcome to my own difficult feelings and experiences for years before I realized my still-hidden desire to have this act of welcome move me past my difficulties to a sense of joy, or to something other than what I was feeling. It was really the line above from Jane Hirshfield's poem that broke it open for me in a deeper way. The still heart, which is what we are trying to cultivate through contemplation, refuses *nothing*.

Contentment doesn't mean we are always happy about life events or deny the reality of pain. We cultivate contentment by cultivating the inner witness who is able to respond to life from a place of calmness, peace, and tranquility. It means we honor that what is given to us in any moment is enough. So it is the "still heart"—the heart of equanimity—that can welcome everything in. Instead of always living with a sense of dissatisfaction about our lives, or anticipation over what comes next, we live in the knowledge that this moment contains everything we need to be at peace, to experience freedom, to develop compassion for ourselves and others, to find God. Benedict's rule counsels contentment with what we have, a sense that what is, is "enough." We don't need anything more and so we are content. When we experience contentment we have softened our bodies, minds, and hearts so that we are able to release the unconscious resistances we hold to our own experience.

We can connect this movement to the practice of simplicity and asceticism that we explored in Chapter Five. Monasticism has always been connected to living simply, but this does not imply bitterness or resentment in the face of scarcity. Instead, the call is to celebrate the sufficiency of what one already has. Contentment is closely connected to the practice of gratitude, of recognizing that having anything is gift. A deep and profound joy is rooted in being content, satisfied with this moment offered to me.

We slow ourselves down as we enter our practice of *lectio divina* and each movement invites us to dive more deeply into the heart of spaciousness. As we transition into the fourth movement we may already be in a place of profound stillness, and yet in *contemplatio* we become even more present and offer ourselves over to its beauty. As we develop our ability to move into the silence of the heart we grow in our capacity to live from this calm center. We are able, more and more, to welcome in all aspects of our experience, even—or especially—in the midst of life's messiness, challenge, and unknowing. We can, as Jane Hirshfield writes in her poem, "refuse nothing." Refusing nothing means making room for the equal measures of sorrow and ecstasy that shower us daily.

The moments when we want to refuse our experience, when we want reality to be other than it is, can be extremely subtle. We may not realize that our gnawing dissatisfaction, or inner resistance, is an act of refusal. Contemplative practice allows us to hear the call to rest into the truth of what is and respond in our daily lives out of our prayer experience. By breathing deeply, we can allow the energy of what we are resisting to have a place in our hearts, and somehow we are able to bear it.

CONTEMPLATION AS A DOORWAY TO TRANSFORMATION

The rush and pressure of modern life are a form,
perhaps the most common form, of its innate violence.

*To allow oneself to be carried away by a multitude
of conflicting concerns, to surrender to too many
demands, to commit oneself to too many projects, to
want to help everyone in everything is to succumb to
violence.*

—*Thomas Merton,* Conjectures of a
Guilty Bystander

These words by Thomas Merton absolutely stopped me in my tracks when I first read them several years ago. Writing here to people who work for peace and justice, he describes the ways in which we participate in our culture's push toward productivity as a mode of participating in its innate violence to our bodies and spirits. Being constantly busy is not only damaging to our body with its need for rest, and our spirit with its need for renewal, but also to society at large. We have become so overwhelmed by life that our ability to discern possible solutions to the complex problems of our age has become severely compromised.

The purpose of contemplative practice is to grow in our presence to God through simply being, rather than trying to *do* anything. When considering the contemplative life, it is important that we don't fall into one of two traps. The first is the belief that contemplation is the purview only of those who have the privilege of time and money, or of those who have joined a contemplative religious order. This belief carries with it a prior judgment about who is capable of contemplative practice and closes it off from the reality of our lives.

The second trap is believing that contemplation will be an antidote to our busy lives and keep us from becoming burned out through overextension. This belief does nothing to address the root causes of our busyness and overreliance on doing. Contemplation is meant to be a doorway to transformation—of ourselves and the culture in which we live—and not just a coping mechanism for tolerating the status quo.

Lectio divina, and the fourth movement of *contemplatio* in particular, can cultivate in us the ability to say a powerful no to the busyness and violence of overdoing in our culture. Through contemplation we are called to a path of deepening awareness of God that brings us closer to our own values and priorities, as well as our sense of communion with others. In this sense, contemplation is not first and foremost a technique for prayer, but a way of being present to what really exists within our own experience. It is the act of taking the time and making space for this presence, and of allowing ourselves to be moved by what we find there. This is the heart of the Benedictine vow of obedience, the act of listening deeply for God in all moments and then responding to what we hear. While contemplation is fundamentally a posture of being and resting into God's presence, if we commit to regular practice, it will inevitably infuse our doing in the world.

Invitation to Practice: Slowing and Stilling

> When the time for silence comes, I ask you to take up your position for prayer (and sitting is usually best for most of us) and then, having asked the help of the Holy Spirit, to be content to wait patiently, expectantly, lovingly, longingly. Try to realize that this is all you can do for yourself. God must do the rest. See yourself as the parched ground looking upwards waiting patiently for the rain to fall. You can only wait.
>
> —Brother Roger of Taize

In this practice allow yourself some extended time to sit in silence. I invite you to pray with one line from Psalm 46:10: "Be still, and know that I am God."

Settling and Shimmering

Begin your time of prayer in your usual way, allowing some time to settle into the space and into your body.

Offer a brief prayer or intention for this time. Bring your awareness to your breath, gently deepening it. Inhaling, imagine the breath of God filling your entire being. Exhaling, imagine yourself releasing thoughts, distractions, and judgments. Continue paying attention to this gentle rhythm of breathing in and breathing out for a few moments. Allow your breath to draw your awareness down to your heart center, placing your hand over your heart to create a physical connection. Breathe in the infinite compassion of God that pulses within you.

Read the phrase for your *lectio* prayer twice slowly. You might even take a full breath between each word to slow yourself down and enter into the mystery of the words:

Be still, and know that I am God.
Be still, and know that I am God.

As the words reverberate in your heart, become aware if one is shimmering before you, asking to be received in a deeper way. Gently repeat this word to yourself in the silence.

Savoring and Stirring
Begin to make room within your heart for any images or memories that arise out of this word. Savor whatever it is that emerges in this time, lingering with it. Make space in your heart center to notice the feelings stirring in response. Continue to breathe, allowing your breath to carry you through the energy of whatever it is you are feeling.

Summoning and Serving
When you feel as though your heart has been touched, shift your awareness to receive whatever call might be emerging in your prayer. Is there a sense of how God might be moving in you now in response to your experience

with this word? Open yourself to receiving the fullness of this call and your own readiness to respond.

Slowing and Stilling

The movement into contemplation means releasing all the words and images that have been in your awareness until now. The other side of sensory prayer, also known as *kataphatic* prayer or the way of images, is *apophatic* prayer, or the way of unknowing, embracing darkness and mystery. This isn't something we do so much as a gift we receive and make ourselves open to. We slow ourselves down even further to allow our hearts to dive deep into this well within us.

Return to the phrase and consider repeating it gently, each time releasing a word:

Be still, and know that I am God *(inhale and exhale)*

Be still, and know that I am *(inhale and exhale)*

Be still, and know *(inhale and exhale)*

Be still *(inhale and exhale)*

Be *(inhale and exhale)*

Continue to be present to the rhythm of your breath, allowing it to be a gentle anchor in the stillness. As thoughts arise, simply notice them with compassion and gently let them go.

Now rest into the great silence of being. Take as much time as you need in this space of stillness and allow your transition out of this time to be gentle, slow, and full of intention.

As you move to the end of your prayer experience it is important to honor that your body and spirit have been in a different place and quality of time. To rush out to the next thing can do violence to ourselves. Make this a conscious movement, allowing your breath to take you from the inner to the outer world. Journaling makes a good transition experience, making time to name what has moved in you and to honor it.

Further Possibilities for Practice

Poetry Exploration: 7-Line Poem

One way to make poetry out of your prayer is to each day write your word or phrase on a slip of paper. At the end of the week put those seven slips of paper in a bowl. Begin with some free writing time to loosen up your pen and connect with your heart. Then select one slip of paper at a time, allowing the words on the paper to be a prompt for the next line of poetry. For example, if I choose the phrase "watered garden" I would incorporate that into the first line of my poem, allowing whatever associations arise to have expression on the page. Then I select the second slip of paper and include that word in the second line. Each line will also be building on the previous one as you create your poem.

Below is an example of a poem that emerged from several different prayer periods. The author said that the exercise helped her see the way her times of prayer were woven together and the larger, deeper image embedded in her experience. The title, "Subiaco," refers to the cave in which St. Benedict first retired from the world and where he later founded the earliest Benedictine monasteries.

Subiaco 2

Yet even now ... return to me.
Stand at the cave entrance
and allow yourself to enter the refuge of my Silence.

Bring your heart of flesh.
Offer your open ear.
Listen to my promises,

and bind them as a sign on your hand.
I who gathered the waters of the sea as in a bottle
will help you hold your heart with all vigilance.

Enter the refuge of my Silence with joy
and you will return to the world with peace.
Out of your newly strengthened vigilant heart
will flow rivers of living water.
Yet even now ... return to me and listen, my child.
    (Judy Smoot)

Suggested Texts for *Lectio Divina*: Silence

Come to me, all you that are weary and are carrying heavy burdens, and I will give you rest. Take my yoke upon you, and learn from me; for I am gentle and humble in heart, and you will find rest for your souls. For my yoke is easy, and my burden is light.

—Matthew 11:28–30

When your tongue is silent, you can rest in the silence of the forest. When your imagination is silent, the forest speaks to you, tells you of its unreality and of the Reality of God. But when your mind is silent, then the forest becomes magnificently real and blazes transparently with the Reality of God.

—Thomas Merton, The Sign of Jonas[4]

We need to find God, and he cannot be found in noise and restlessness. God is the friend of silence. See how nature—trees, flowers, grass—grows in silence; see the stars, the moon, and the sun, how they move in silence. We need silence to be able to touch souls.

—*Mother Teresa*

Silence is painful, but in silence things take form, and we must wait and watch. In us, in our secret depth, lies the knowing element which sees and hears that which we do not see nor hear. All our perceptions, all the things we have done, all that we are today, dwelt once in that knowing, silent depth, that treasure chamber in the soul. And we are more than we think. We are more than we know. That which is more than we think and know is always seeking and adding to itself while we are doing—or think we are doing nothing. But to be conscious of what is going on in our depth is to help it along. When subconsciousness becomes consciousness, the seeds in our winter-clad selves turn to flowers, and the silent life in us sings with all its might.

—*Kahlil Gibran*[5]

Why are you so afraid of silence,
silence is the root of everything.
If you spiral into its void,
a hundred voices will thunder messages you long to
    hear.

—*Rumi*, Hidden Music

Of secret things I am silence, of the wise I am the wisdom. Furthermore, O Arjuna, I am the generating seed of all existences. There is no being—moving or nonmoving—that can exist without me. O mighty conqueror of enemies, there is no end to my divine manifestations. What I have spoken to you is but a mere indication of my infinite opulences.

—*Bhaghavad Gita, texts 38–40*

For Reflection

Are there specific times of day when you seek to drown out silence? What is it about these times that draws you into busyness and noise?

What are the images and sensory experiences that you associate with God?

Describe a time in your life when self-judgment or self-criticism stopped you from pursuing something you wanted to pursue.

PART THREE

Reading the World

VISIO DIVINA

Praying with Images

*The real voyage of discovery consists not in seeking
new landscapes, but in having new eyes.*

—*Marcel Proust*

The four movements of *lectio* create a sacred rhythm that nurtures our ability to experience God's presence in the world around us. As we grow in our ability to become present to God in our prayer, this awareness begins to spill over into our daily lives. We may discover that more and more often we have moments of grace and insight that bubble up throughout the day. This expanding vision is one of the fruits of this practice, as *lectio divina* invites us to slowly widen the possibilities for sacred texts. One of the fundamental assumptions of *lectio divina* is that the Divine Presence is everywhere, and we can apply its principles to praying visually with art as well. Rather than listening for the sacred word or phrase that calls to us, in *visio divina* we look for an image or a symbol or a color. In essence, we pray with our eyes.

ART AS A DOORWAY OF THE DIVINE

Every religious tradition honors the role of art as a vehicle for transcendent experience. The most immediate way we become aware of this is in houses of worship. The architecture and design of churches, synagogues, and mosques are crafted in such a way as to create an experience of a building as a sacred vessel. When we approach a house of worship, there is a sense that we are entering space transfigured. God is not more present in these places than in others, but our awareness of the Sacred Presence is often heightened because of the intention and attention to form and beauty. Frescoes and sculpture, minarets and domes, intensely colored stained glass, and intricately carved wooden doors are intended to inspire wonder and awe at the magnificence of creation. Even the simplicity and sparseness of a Quaker meeting house has its own kind of aesthetic meant to cultivate and support an encounter with God.

Icons are another form of art often associated with sacred purpose. The term *icon* comes from the Greek word *eikona*, which simply means "image," but icons are more than mere images. The theological foundation for the use of icons rests in Scripture: the Christian scriptures describes Christ as the *eikon*— the image and exact representation of God (Hebrews 1:3). The Orthodox say that an icon is written rather than painted, and speak of icon writers rather than icon painters. Icons as they are used in Orthodox liturgy and prayer life are no more objects of worship than the pages, ink, and typeface of a prayer book. The Orthodox believer prays *through*, not to, an icon, reverencing not the icon itself but the sacred person or scene it represents. In addition to depicting Christ and the Trinity, icons also portray Mary, the mother of Jesus, and the saints. Several years ago, after my mother died, someone gave me an icon of the *Theokotos*, which is the Greek title for Mary and means God-bearer, "one who gives birth to God." In this icon she holds the Christ child in her arms and her cheek is pressed up against his. There they dwell, cheek to cheek, in an act of deep intimacy. I kept this on my altar for several months and it became a doorway for me to reverence God as Mother, who comforts me in my sorrow and is the bearer of new life.

Similarly in Hindu tradition, *murti* are images that express a divine spirit. The word literally means "embodiment," and they can be crafted from different materials, such as stone, metal, and wood. *Murti* are considered more than an expression of the Divine, but an incarnation or manifestation of the God-taken form.

It is not just artwork as form that has spiritual significance for prayer. In traditions like Buddhism, creating art is a way to teach and practice foundational spiritual principles. For example, flower arranging and calligraphy are spiritual practices that apply the art of simplicity. Intricate mandalas are created from colored sand and then the wind is allowed to blow them away as a meditation on impermanence and the practice of nonattachment. This act of letting go is also a profound act of humility.

PRAYING WITH THE EYES OF THE HEART

May the eyes of your hearts be enlightened.
—Ephesians 1:18

Benedict begins his rule by calling us to listen with the "ears of our hearts." Much of *lectio divina* is grounded in this fundamental act of reverential listening, of learning to hear the undercurrents and movements of the heart. But in Paul's letter to the Ephesians, we find the image of the "eyes of the heart" offered to us as well. He is praying for a spiritual awakening, that we may see things previously hidden to us. If in biblical and mystical traditions the heart is the seat of our whole being, then to see with the heart means we are invited to see the world with the whole of ourselves. The prayer of gazing is looking upon something with the eyes of the heart, a soft, receptive way of being with an image.

If our eyes are functioning normally, we spend most of our waking life seeing the world around us and in front of us. We look for things and respond to visual cues in our environment. Spiritual seeing, however, is different than the hard stare of our daily lives, where our eyes are in service of whatever goal we are working toward in the moment, whether driving to work, reading a computer screen, or seeing what is in the refrigerator for dinner. Franciscan priest Richard Rohr describes spiritual seeing as if "there is another pair of eyes inside of me seeing through me, seeing with me, seeing in me. God can see God everywhere, and God in me can see God everywhere." The fourteenth-century German mystic Meister Eckhart expressed it this way: "The eye with which I see God is the same with which God sees me. My eye and God's eye is one eye, and one sight, and one knowledge, and one love." If we embrace what we learned about heart-centered prayer, we acknowledge that the heart is the place of our full encounter with the Divine Presence within each of us. To see with the eyes of the heart means to see the world from God's perspective—to see holiness pulsing everywhere.

Depending on the translation, the word *behold* appears more than a thousand times in Scripture. It is the most common translation for the Hebrew word *hinneh* and the Greek word *idou*. Both of these words mean something like "Pay close attention to what follows—it is important!" There is no other word in English that conveys this meaning, although "Look!" and "See!" express a similar energy. When we behold something, we approach it with awe and reverence, see it with eyes wide open, and take in the depths of what is presented to us. Practicing *visio divina* helps us cultivate our ability to behold the sacred in the world around us.

I engage in the practice of praying with the eyes of the heart through photography. I have loved photography for many years, but it wasn't until I immersed myself in monastic practice that I discovered it as a tool for contemplation. Photography helps me cultivate my ability to slow down and see the sacred shimmering in the world. Photography can be a form of contemplative prayer when we engage it as a way of seeing, and I teach photography classes so others can learn a more heart-centered approach to receiving images, rather than simply "taking" them.

CHOOSING AN IMAGE FOR VISIO DIVINA

I invite you into the practice of *visio divina* with a favorite piece of art. There is an icon by artist and iconographer Heather Williams Durka on page 151.[1] You can begin with that or choose any piece of art that calls to you.

There are a number of ways you might select an image with which to pray. You might begin with one of the traditional Orthodox icons from Christian traditions or search online or for books with images of art from different religious traditions. I recommend finding a book such as *Meditating with Mandalas* by David Fontana, which offers mandala art from a variety of religious traditions. Mandalas were created for the purpose of deeper contemplation. Or ask a spiritual director for a recommendation.

You might also select a favorite piece of art, such as *Starry Night* by Vincent Van Gogh or *The Kiss* by Gustav Klimt, and allow those to be an entry into prayer. Or notice when you find a photograph that makes you gasp at its beauty, and save it to pray with later. If you encounter a piece of art that repels you, on the other hand, consider bringing it to prayer to discover what the strong emotional response might reveal to you about how God is working in your life.

Invitation to Practice: Visio Divina

On entering into myself I saw, as if it were with the eyes of my soul, what was beyond the eyes of the soul, beyond my spirit: your immutable light.

—Augustine of Hippo, Confessions X

Praying visually is a different experience than praying with a text. For some, it feels more natural and for others, less so. See whether you can approach the experience with an open heart and allow it to be a journey of discovery.

Settling and Shimmering

Close your eyes and prepare yourself for prayer by connecting to your body and breath, gently deepening the rhythm of your breath, bringing your awareness to your heart center. As you breathe in, imagine receiving the gift of vision, the sacred ability to see deeply below the surface of things. As you breathe out, imagine being able to allow your eyes to communicate love to others and to what you gaze upon. Allow a few moments to rest into this nourishing rhythm of preparing your eyes to behold what is before you.

Gently open your eyes and gaze upon your chosen icon softly with "the eyes of the heart." This is a gentle, receptive gaze, not a hard, penetrating stare. Move your eyes over the image, taking in all of its colors, shapes, and symbols. Bring a sense of curiosity to this image, exploring it with reverence, noticing all of its textures and features that come with seeing more closely.

As your eyes wander around the image in a brief visual pilgrimage, notice if there is a particular area or feature of the icon that draws your attention, that stirs energy for you. Allow your eyes to rest gently there.

Savoring and Stirring

Be present to this place on the icon that is calling for more attention. Open your imagination to memories and other images that want to stir in you in response. Allow this place, these symbols or colors, to unfold, to make other connections. Savor what emerges. Notice if there are any feelings rising within you. Connect to your breath

again, making room for whatever wants to move through you in this time.

Summoning and Serving

As the icon moves your heart, listen for how you are being invited in this moment of your life out of this time of prayer. Make space for your heart to be touched and for a longing to respond to God's call to move in you. The invitation may emerge as an image or a symbol instead of as words. Ask how your life is becoming a work of art, and how you are called to claim your place as artist of this masterpiece. Where in your life are you called to bring more color, to bring more mystery? Explore what the artwork of your life wants you to discover.

Slowing and Stilling

Close your eyes if they are still open and release the images you have been gazing upon. Sink into stillness, slow your breath down, and rest in the grace of being for several minutes.

When you are ready to end your time of prayer, connect with your breath again and gently bring your awareness back to the room. In maintaining eyes of the heart, sometimes it can be helpful to gaze upon the image one more time—following your prayer, taking the image in again, and seeing if you notice anything new. Then offer a moment of gratitude for the way this image has touched your heart.

Further Possibilities for Practice

Art Exploration: Collage

Collage is one of my favorite mediums because it is so accessible and very powerful. It is an especially meaningful way to work with symbols in a simple and nonthreatening way. The act of bringing together a variety of images into a whole can create a sense of inner unity and stillness. Often when I gaze upon the completed collage, I look for the meaning in the way the images rest close together or far apart, or for what the combination of images and colors reveals about my thinking process when the art was made.

Collage requires only a few simple tools: a piece of heavy paper, a glue stick, and images. Magazines work well, although I have started buying used art books on sale and relishing the experience of tearing out the pages; the paper also tends to be sturdier. I suggest taking just one magazine and limiting yourself to the images you find there and also setting a time limit. I also suggest the heavy paper you use for the base be a small size, say 6 x 6 inches square, or any size that feels satisfying to you. The limits on the size of the paper, the number of magazines, and your time create a helpful structure for the experience. I can get lost in making collages for hours, but sometimes when I move through the experience with limits in place, it helps me release my inner critic more easily. A half hour is enough time and the framework can help move you past your resistance and judgments.

I offer here two possible ways of working with collage and *lectio divina*.

Collage as a Response to a *Lectio* Prayer Experience

Here is a way for your work with collage to be a deepening of your *lectio divina* experience with a sacred text. It takes place at the conclusion of a *lectio divina* session, as a fifth movement.

Gather together your supplies and approach this time as a continuation of your prayer. Begin this process by centering yourself and offering an intention, such as opening your heart to deeper wisdom around your *lectio divina* experience. Gently hold the word or phrase that shimmered for you in your *lectio divina* session, and allow it to be a touchstone in your process. Connect again to your breath and heart. As you inhale, whisper your word or phrase and allow it to fill you; as you exhale, release it. Rest into this rhythm of breath for a few moments. Then enter into this time of art-making, releasing expectations of what will be revealed. If you already have images in your mind that you are looking for, see if you can release those as well.

As you flip through the pages of the magazine or art book, resist the urge to read the articles and simply notice which images stir an energetic response in you. This might be an experience of resonance or dissonance, similar to the process of listening for the word or phrase that shimmers for you in *lectio divina*. Tear out the pages and then gather several images together. Either by tearing or using scissors, whittle the image down to the element you want to bring to your collage. Arrange these elements on the heavy paper in a way that feels satisfying. Try not to think this through. Simply allow the process to unfold. Be present to inner voices that rise up and, through your breath, simply let them go. Glue the images down.

After you have finished, allow some time to be present to what has emerged. You might engage in some journaling and reflect on the experience you have when gazing upon this collage. Gazing means bringing soft and receptive eyes to the images.

Visio Divina with Your Collage

Another possible way to engage *lectio divina* is to bring the process of *visio divina*, which we explored above with the icon, to your completed collage. This time, allow yourself to gaze upon the collage and receive its images and symbols. Notice if there is a particular detail shimmering for you that wants deeper attention. Allow it to unfold in your imagination, tending to the feelings it stirs. Then listen for the invitation it offers to you. This can be a powerful and reverential way of being with the art you have created from a place of prayer. Bring your loving eyes to your own creation and honor it as sacred text in its own right, with gifts to offer you again and again.

Art Exploration: Mandala

A meaningful way to give expression to your *lectio divina* practice in visual form is by creating a mandala. *Mandala* is the Sanskrit word for "circle" and serves as a symbol for wholeness across traditions and cultures. The circle is an ancient and archetypal image, found in rose windows, labyrinths, and the spirals of ancient Celtic symbols. Psychologist Carl Jung created a mandala each day out of his dream images as a way of honoring the symbols stirring in his imagination.

I invite you to create a mandala in response to your *lectio divina* experience. All you need is paper and colored pens. Draw a circle. You can draw it free-form, use a compass, or trace the bottom of a large jar or pan onto the paper. With some markers, crayons, or colored pencils, move into a time of drawing in response to your experience of stillness. Allow the circle to be a sacred container for your prayer and just notice which images and colors want to emerge. You might gently hold your word or phrase from prayer, or perhaps the invitation that emerged, and allow your art to explore it.

Another way to enter into the fourth movement of *lectio divina* through art is to fill with color a mandala form that has already been created for you. In Appendix 3, you will find a black-and-white mandala shared by artist Stacy Wills that you can copy and use for this purpose.[2]

Consider moving through your *lectio divina* practice in your usual way, but when you come to the time of contemplation, turn to your mandala and your tools for coloring. Without thinking it through, select the colors that draw you and allow this to be a meditative experience. Stay connected to your breath as you enter into this deep visual prayer of what is found in silence.

For Reflection

What is your favorite piece of art and what is it about the work that draws you to it?

Which colors bring you alive?

Are there ways in which your eyes could be renewed to see the world more deeply?

What would it mean for you to consider your own life a work of art in progress?

AUDIO DIVINA

Praying with Sound

*Therefore let everyone who understands God by faith
faithfully offer Him tireless praise, and with joyful
devotion sing to Him without ceasing.*
            —*Hildegard of Bingen*, Scivias

This chapter explores music as another sacred text through which we can encounter the Holy. Augustine of Hippo famously wrote in his commentary on the psalms, "He who sings, prays twice." The psalms themselves are filled with descriptions of singing to God, such as "I will sing praise to your name" (9:2) and "Praise him with tambourine and dance; praise him with strings and pipe!" (150:4). All of creation is commanded to sing out: "Make a joyful noise to the Lord, all the earth. Worship the Lord with gladness; come into his presence with singing" (100:1–2). Music is primordial sound, a powerful art form that has the capacity to stir the emotions and charge our memory.

    The teachers at the yoga studio in Seattle where I practice regularly begin and end class with the sacred sound of Om, as is traditional in yoga. There is a moment of great beauty when we enter into the vibration of the class together. The vibrations that emerge from my body and join with the vibrations of others is a powerful experience of community through music. In *The Call of the Upanishads*, Rohit Mehta writes that Om:

> indicates the coexistence of the articulate and the inarticulate sounds—of the heard and unheard melodies—of the sound that is struck and the sound that is unstruck, the *Anahata Nada*.... Sound obviously consists of vibrations, and all vibrations have a beginning and an end. But if there could be a sound which is unstruck—the *Anahata Nada*—then surely there could be no end to it as there is no beginning to it. To talk of a vibration-less sound is indeed to indulge in a paradox. In the sacred word Om, there is such a paradox. It is both heard and unheard, struck as well as unstruck. It is both perishable and imperishable.[1]

The *anahata,* or "heart chakra," is responsible for the reception of the internal music, but not in the way of a normal sensory organ. You can listen deeply to your own inner sound through the ear of the heart, which leads to a process of spiritual awakening. The deeper you experience this primal vibration within the heart, the more you can experience it as penetrating all matter, vibrating eternally throughout creation.

In yogic belief, ultimate reality emanates from the primordial "first sound," the imperceptible vibration that gives rise to the universe. The entire physical world, including human beings, is a materialization of the different frequencies of this root vibrational energy. This sound is the universal pulse of life and creation and is manifested within us as the sound of our own heart beating. For thousands of years, this primal beat has been expressed by the beat of the drum.

The image from the Upanishads of sound energy as the fundamental creative force that is without beginning and end is similar in concept to the opening words of the Gospel of John: "In the beginning was the Word, and the Word was with God, and the Word was God" (1:1). Similarly, in the first creation story of the Hebrew Bible, God "speaks" creation into being: "Then God said, 'Let there be light'; and there was light" (Genesis 1:3). The rhythm of this creation account—"And God said"—calls us to remember a God whose deepest song and sound utters us into being. We contain that sound within us. So when we enter into prayer of the heart through *lectio divina*, allowing the different sounds and rhythms of this universal music to be the text of our prayer, we are called into relationship with the God who sings to us and through us.

PRAYING THE HOURS IN CHRISTIAN MONASTIC TRADITION

The practice of the liturgy of the hours, a service of psalms, hymns, and Scripture readings, is an ancient one in Christian spirituality. The original purpose of saying the hours at eight fixed times throughout the day, from Matins to Compline, was to pray continuously, returning again and again to an awareness of the Sacred Presence throughout the day. Benedict, in writing his rule, devotes several sections to guidelines for keeping this prayer at the heart of the community. In the medieval church there were eight traditional prayer offices, or hours, although today most monastic communities have simplified this to four. For many liturgical Christians, including Roman Catholics, Lutherans, and Episcopalians, the main prayer times are those of morning and evening—traditionally called lauds and vespers.

The practice of praying the hours actually originated in Jewish tradition; according to Psalm 119, "Seven times a day do I praise you." It is believed to be, along with the eucharist, one of the earliest forms of prayer in which the Christian community engaged. In the cities of the Roman Empire, a bell would ring every three hours to keep work orderly and signal when breaks were to be taken. Every part of daily life became ordered by these bells, including Jewish and then Christian prayer. Gradually, during the first century of the Common Era, praying the daily office became more formal, practiced not only in small gatherings of Christians but also alone and in families and extended households. In the third century the desert mothers and fathers, those earliest monastics, wanted to follow St. Paul's invitation to "pray without ceasing." In communities, they would pass the praying of an office from one group of monks to another, creating a continuous cascade of prayer.

In his rule, St. Benedict structured monastic life around the praying of the hours. The word *office* comes from the Latin word *opus*, or "work," and thus praying the hours was also known as *opus dei*, the work of God. Benedict's rule is based on the principle of *ora et labora*, a balance of work and prayer. Thus, when we pray we are participating in divine work; when we work, we are participating in prayer. For Benedict, every moment contained an invitation to sacred awareness. The psalms form the core of the prayers, and some monastic communities used to sing all 150 in the course of a day. Now it is more usual to move through the cycle over a course of anywhere from one to eight weeks or more, depending on the frequency of the offices.

Hildegard of Bingen, the great Benedictine abbess of the twelfth century, composed a great deal of music to be used in praying the liturgy of the hours. We are fortunate to have many fine recordings available to us of her work. She believed that music originated from a primordial and celestial source, and so the practice of singing the hours was a way of joining in with this eternal choir. Hildegard considered this form of prayer to be even more essential than the eucharist to the formation of her community. She writes, "Music arouses the sluggish soul to watchfulness. It has power to soften even hard hearts, and by rendering hearts moist it ushers in the Holy Spirit. Through the power of hearing, God opens to human beings all the glorious sounds of the hidden mysteries and of the choirs of angels by whom God is praised over and over again" (*Scivias* I, 4.18). Music softens our hearts so that we can make space for the Spirit to enter and we can join with the "hidden mysteries." The music we sing is only a dim reflection of the heavenly choirs, the music from before the Fall, which we could not hear in our earthly condition.

CHOOSING MUSIC

As with texts and art, there is no shortage of possible music for prayer. I suggest you begin with instrumental music for the sake of simplicity, because lyrics add another layer of complexity to pay attention to. I am very fond of the "Sarabande" movements from Bach's *Solo Suites for Cello* with their slow tempo and deep vibrations, which I experience as music of the heart.

You can choose any piece of music with which to pray. I suggest something around three to five minutes, because you will be repeating it. Classical music offers rich resources and you might experiment with small chamber or large symphony orchestras, seeing which you respond to best.

There is also a wide variety of chant music with which you could pray—Gregorian chant, Hindu chants and kirtans, and Sufi chants. Notice whether the inclusion of lyrics with the music is distracting to your prayer or whether it assists you in diving more deeply.

Contemporary secular music is also an appropriate source, especially if there is a song you already love and you want to experience it in a new way. If you are like me, you already practice a form of *audio divina* when you find that favorite song and play it over and over again, allowing it to shape your soul. You might also pray with a song that brings you back to a particular event or season of your life. It may be a song that comes on the radio and suddenly you find yourself emotionally connected to another time and place. Praying *audio divina* will give some space to honor those memories that are being stirred.

Invitation to Practice: *Audio Divina*

> *Entering the human heart, [God's] divine touch*
> *sets its strings vibrating. [God] draws from them a*
> *variety of sounds, from zeal to compunction,*
> *which blends into a marvelous spiritual sym-*
> *phony. Between the sacred author, moved by*
> *the Spirit to write the text, and the reader,*
> *moved by the same Spirit when reading it, a*
> *deep communion is established. Time's differ-*
> *ences do not matter because both are in com-*
> *munion with the Word of the living God.*
> —Mariano Magrassi, Praying the Bible:
> Introduction to *Lectio Divina*

I invite you to practice *audio divina*, or sacred hearing, with a piece of music you have chosen. Like *visio divina*, this experience is at first more natural for some to enter into than others.

Settling and Shimmering

Prepare yourself for prayer by connecting to your body and breath. Music is deeply connected to our physical experience because we feel its vibrations in our bodies. The steady rhythm of heart and breath connect us to the rise and fall of music. There are spaces that lend them-selves especially well to acoustics. As you breathe in, imagine a wide open space being hollowed out within you as a sacred chamber in which to listen to the music. As you breathe out, release whatever stands in your way of being present to the gift of music in this time.

Gently bring your awareness to your heart center. Open yourself to hearing with the ears of your heart. Music calls us to a kind of attunement. Listening to words and speech has a different quality than does hearing song. There is an embodiment of the experience that reveals aspects of the Holy to us in the process.

Play the piece you have selected through once or twice. As you listen, see if you can bring your awareness into your body and really experience the music and its vibrations and resonances within you.

As you listen, notice if there is an image, a feeling, or even a sound that shimmers. Because it is music, especially if it is instrumental, the "word" may come in another form. Open your heart to receiving what that may be. Trust however you are moved, and allow that response to be the entrance point for your prayer.

Savoring and Stirring

Play the music again and this time allow the word, image, or feeling to unfold within you, in that open space you have created interiorly. Allow your imagination to spread wide open and be present to all that stirs in your heart. Notice if there are any memories being evoked.

Music often evokes a strong emotional response, so take special care to welcome in the feelings that rise up in you and allow them to have the fullness of space within you. Notice how your feelings rise and fall with the music itself. After the piece is finished playing, rest in the silence for a few moments, connecting to how your body is responding.

Summoning and Serving

You may want to play the music one more time. In the silence that follows, listen for how you are being called through this prayer experience to respond. Is there an invitation being extended to you?

How is your life like a song or a symphony? Are there ways for you to make yourself more open to the music God wants to play in your heart?

Slowing and Stilling

Turn off the music and take some time to sit in silence, feeling the resonance in your body, releasing all thought.

Rest into this space of stillness and being, attuning yourself to the hum of creation in harmony with the rhythm of your breath.

As you close, notice if there is a song stirring in you or a tune you are feeling moved to hum. Just allow whatever expression wants to come through in this time. If words would be helpful, take some time to journal about your experience.

Further Possibilities for Practice

Heartbeat of *Lectio*

If in the Upanishads the heartbeat is an expression of the primordial sound from which all creation emerged, and in Christian tradition the heart is where we encounter a God who spoke everything into being, then a prayer of simply being present to the beat of your heart can be a profound experience. We practiced heart-centered prayer in Chapter Two. Here I invite you to engage *lectio divina* with this music within you.

Rest into silence and place your hand over your heart or your fingers on your pulse. In a way similar to the form of *audio divina* outlined in this chapter, see if the music of your heart can carry you through the four movements of *lectio divina*. As you connect to your pulse, what are the words or images that shimmer and rise up? What are you aware of? Is there an invitation that emerges from this simple prayer? Close with some time to rest into stillness and then call into your awareness the beating of hearts all through creation. Allow your own heartbeat to be a doorway into honoring the life essence of all persons and creatures. Then honor the rhythm of the sea, the phases of the moon, and the rising and setting of the sun that also reflect this primal pulse. You might want to close with some gentle drumming as a way to reflect this rhythm back to the world.

Toning

> I teach my sighs to lengthen into songs.
> —Theodore Roethke

"Toning" is the act of creating extended vocal sounds with a single vowel in order to experience the sound and its vibrations throughout the body. There is no worry of following a melody or harmony, no words to remember, no rhythm to follow. Toning is just the act of softening the jaw and opening the throat so that the vibration of breath can emerge in sound. You can experiment by toning with each of the main vowel sounds: a-e-i-o-u. Let each one be an extended sound and increase the tone to feel the vibration in your body strengthen.

You can tone while sitting or standing or lying down. Experiment with toning while you walk or engage in an everyday task. Play with the vibrations in your body when making a sustained sound. Open your mouth and create an openness in your throat. Begin toning a sound—it could be the Hindu primal sound of Om, or it could be one of the vowel sounds that emerges in your playful experimentation.

Create a sound and hold its resonance. Consider beginning and ending your *lectio divina* practice with a sacred sound or song. Ring a chime to bring sound into your regular practice.

Chant

Chanting can build from toning. In toning you are experimenting with sound and vibration. In chanting you choose a word or phrase and give it expression through breath and tone and sound. You might want to play with the word or phrase that shimmered in your *lectio divina* practice with sacred text to find an accompanying sound. Sing it aloud, experimenting with single notes or a scale that rises or falls. Create a chant from your prayer, keeping it simple and playful. As you express the word that shimmers in this way, what do you discover as it vibrates through your being?

Taize is an ecumenical monastic community founded in France where a great deal of contemporary chant music has been composed. Taize services can be found in most cities, with chants staying consistent from place to place. A cherished memory from some time I spent in Vienna was gathering for a Taize service in St. Rupert's, the oldest church in the city center. A blaze of candles was lit to illuminate our hearts as we entered into song together. Sometimes one of the lines of chant comes back to me while I am walking or on retreat. I will then pray *lectio divina* with it, singing it again and again, listening for how it moves my heart and what invitation is hidden there for me. As my mother lay dying in the hospital, the chants from Taize rose up again and again from my throat to bathe her in song.

An excellent resource for learning to chant is Cynthia Bourgeault's *Chanting the Psalms*.

For Reflection

Name significant times in your life when, as you reflect back on them, you remember sounds in particular. What are the sounds—music, voices, beats—that mark those memories?

Are there songs that immediately call to mind a particular moment in time for you, or a season of your life?

Have you ever been lost in music, whether playing music or listening to music? Describe the setting and sounds.

CHAPTER ELEVEN

NATURE AS SACRED TEXT

Every being is praising God
The fire has its flame and praises God.
The wind blows the flame and praises God.
In the voice we hear the word which praises God.
And the word, when heard, praises God.
So all of creation is a song of praise to God.
—*Hildegard of Bingen*, Scivias

This chapter explores nature as a sacred text, a source for *lectio divina* and place of revelation. Nature has been traditionally considered one of the two primary "books" of revelation, with Scripture as the other. Creation is the primal text of revelation, with God's creative birthing imprinted on every element, while nature is the very matrix of our existence. Without her gifts, we would not be able to sustain our lives. If we return to *audio divina*'s insight about the primordial sound vibrating through all of creation, it seems a natural extension to find mystics and saints joining this song of praise heard through fire and wind, as celebrated by Hildegard of Bingen. In the nineteenth-century Russian Orthodox book *The Way of the Pilgrim*, the author writes:

And while I prayed in the depths of the heart, everything around me seemed transformed: the trees, grass, birds, earth, air, light—every created thing seemed to proclaim that it bears witness to God's love for humanity. Everything was praying. Everything sang glory be to God! I also understood what the *Philokalia* calls, "a knowledge of the language of all creation," and I saw how it was possible to converse with God's creatures.[1]

We find this exuberant, ecstatic awareness of the overflowing of creation in a song of praise from Psalm 19:

> The heavens are telling the glory of God;
> and the firmament proclaims his handiwork.
> Day to day pours forth speech,
> and night to night declares knowledge.
> There is no speech, nor are there words;
> their voice is not heard;
> yet their voice goes out through all the earth,
> and their words to the end of the world.
>
> —*Psalm 19:1–4*

Each morning I go on a long walk among the trees in a nearby park. This is a form of *lectio divina* I practice with nature as the sacred text, revealing holy wonders to my heart. I move across the silence of grass, near the autumn explosion of dahlias, and on to the lush and extravagant gesture of ferns. If I listen closely I can hear the steady hum of trees breathing, a song of adoration whispered from outstretched branches. I am invited to join my own voice to this choir and sing a holy yes to what I hear.

Consider when you pray through chant, toning, or song that you are joining your voice to the unending hymn of praise already resounding through creation at every moment.

ALLOWING NATURE TO TEACH US TO PRAY

> *Believe me as one who has experience, you will find*
> *much more among the woods than ever you will*
> *among books. Woods and stones will teach you what*
> *you can never hear from any master.*
> —*Saint Bernard of Clairvaux,* Letters

In the opening pages of *Being Still: Reflections on an Ancient Mystical Tradition*, Jean-Yves Leloup describes a young philosopher who comes to a hermit on Mt. Athos, Fr. Seraphim, and asks to learn the prayer of the heart. Fr. Seraphim replies that before he teaches the philosopher this way of prayer, he must learn to meditate like a mountain: "And he showed him an enormous rock. 'Ask it how it goes about praying. Then come back to me.'"[2] So the young man learns stability of posture and grounding from the mountain, the weight of presence, and the experience of calm. He enters into the timeless time of mountains and experiences eternity within and around him, while also learning the grace of the seasons.

Next, Fr. Seraphim sends the young philosopher to learn how to meditate like a poppy, taking his mountain wisdom with him. From the poppy he learns to turn himself toward the light and to orient his meditation practice from his inner depths toward radiance. The poppy also teaches him both uprightness and the ability to bend with the wind. And while the mountain teaches him about the eternal, the poppy teaches him about the finitude of our days as the blossom begins to wither. He learns that meditation means experiencing the eternal in each fleeting moment.

The young man is then sent to the ocean to observe the wisdom of ebbing and flowing, and he learns to synchronize his breath with the "great breathing rhythm of the waves." As he floats on the water he discovers the great calmness of the sea below its undulating surface and learns to hold awareness of his own distinct self without being carried away by the rhythm of breathing.

Next Fr. Seraphim has him learn to pray like a bird, telling him that the prophet Isaiah describes meditation as the cry of an animal, like a roaring lion or the song of a dove. The bird is to teach him how to sing continuously, repeating the name of God in his heart without ceasing. The invocation of the divine name leads him to a deep place of stillness.

In the last two movements in this story, the young man is told to learn to meditate like Abraham and embrace the practice of hospitality, freeing his heart of the need to judge others. Finally he is instructed to meditate like Jesus, who is the one who knows how to pray like a mountain, a poppy, an ocean, and a bird, and who exemplifies the boundless love of Abraham. Jesus is the one who calls God Abba, and the final lesson is to await the time when "Abba" emerges from the depths of his heart spontaneously. For the rest of the young man's life,

> when he was feeling agitated or pressed for time, he would sit like a mountain. Whenever he felt pride or conceit, he would remember the poppy, that "every flower withers." When sadness, anger, or disgust overtook him, he would breathe deeply like the ocean and rediscover his own breath in the breath of God, invoking God's name and crying softly, "*Kyrie eleison.*"[3]

In Buddhism we find the principle of interdependence can also offer an ecological vision that integrates all aspects of creation in recognizing our mutuality and interdependence. Buddhist teachings state that all things are interconnected. There is nothing in existence that is separate, fixed, or isolated. Things only exist in relationship and connection with other things. In this web of interconnection we discover that Buddhism honors nature as teacher as well:

Like the Buddha, we too should look around us and be observant, because everything in the world is ready to teach us. With even a little intuitive wisdom we will be able to see clearly through the ways of the world. We will come to understand that everything in the world is a teacher. Trees and vines, for example, can all reveal the true nature of reality. With wisdom there is no need to question anyone, no need to study. We can learn from Nature enough to be enlightened, because everything follows the way of Truth. It does not diverge from Truth.[4]

I have always considered my dogs to be my primary spiritual directors. Currently, we have a wise dog named Winter in our home who offers me daily wisdom in learning how to simply be present to the truth of this moment. She reminds me to follow the sacred rhythms of my body through the day. We live in an anthropocentric world, and our churches are no better. We have lost sight of the tremendous gift of wisdom creatures have to offer us, simply by virtue of their "otherness." Animals don't spend their lives, as far as I know, trying to rationalize and think through things, making important plans. Their gifts of instinctual and intuitive being, love, and care invite us into a bigger way of being ourselves. We could learn a great deal by becoming a disciple of trees and birds, of sitting at their feet as in the story of Fr. Seraphim, and learning what they have to teach us about presence and prayer.

Invitation to Practice: *Lectio Divina* with Nature

Seek not revelations, all is revealed.
Listen to each word, a world in orbit;
each phrase, a nova: essay the beach,
each grain of sand, a poem.
—Marilyn Buck, "Revelation"

I invite you to pray *lectio divina* with nature and suggest you bring the rhythm and movements of your *lectio* practice with you out on a walk. Go to a place of natural beauty, the woods or a beach. Even a neighborhood park can serve the process well. This is a regular practice of mine, to walk in a contemplative way and listen for what is shimmering for me out in the world and how it is speaking to me of the Divine.

Settling and Shimmering

Before you go outside, allow a few moments to ground and center yourself. During this time of walking, remember that you aren't trying to get anywhere, but simply exploring the world in an openhearted and prayerful way. Connect with your breath, inhaling and filling with the life-giving breath of God, and exhaling, releasing your plans and expectations for this time and allowing yourself to simply receive whatever happens as gift. Consider offering a brief blessing for this experience.

As you walk, bring your full attention and presence to each step. Allow your breath to be full and deep. Bring the soft gaze you were invited to practice with art and icons in *visio divina* to the world around you. As you move through the world, listen and look. Notice if there is something shimmering in the world and calling for your deeper attention. Perhaps it is a leaf or flower, the bark of a tree or a wide-open vista. Slow yourself down even more and simply linger with this landscape or object in nature that has become your word or phrase.

Savoring and Stirring

As you gaze upon this object, open your heart to any images, memories, or feelings that stir in response to it, welcoming in whatever comes. Allow a few moments of presence to the way it is speaking to you in this moment.

Summoning and Serving

Begin to ask yourself what the invitation might be here for you. Make space for the response to rise up. How is God calling you to be in response to what you see? How do you walk in the world? How do you long to walk in the world?

Then connect again to your breath, and continue to walk and listen. Look for the next thing to capture your heart in this moment and move through this process again. Repeat this as many times as you feel led.

Slowing and Stilling

When you return from your walk, allow a few moments to simply sit in stillness, being present to your body's energy. Notice how your body feels after this time of movement and presence. Close with a few minutes of journaling and naming your experience.

I often pray in this way on my daily morning walks. They are a time for me to slow my thoughts down, focus on my body, and be present to the world in a heart-centered way.

Further Possibilities for Practice

Nature as Icon

Gazing is an act of loving reverence, a way of seeing that opens us up to being transformed. We live in such a visual culture that our attention is caught and held by hundreds of images every day, but how often do we really see? Nature is an icon, a sacred image that slowly shifts beneath my gaze, revealing a God who is constantly creating. As I sit in nature I not only become aware of a Holy Presence at work in the world around me, the Great Artist, but I also begin to connect deeply to the Divine slowly at work within me, crafting and shaping my life, inviting me here this day to sit in stillness and witness the beauty of the world. Nature invites us to linger, to relish, to be in awe. I imagine those ancient poets who wrote the psalms of creation, celebrating God's grandeur and mystery.

As an alternative to the walking *lectio divina* practice offered above, if you find yourself in a place where you simply want to take in the landscape before you, consider praying *visio divina* following the guidelines in Chapter Nine for this way of practice. You might want to pick up a few natural objects—stones, twigs, acorns, some dried grass—on which to meditate at home. And if you don't have easy access to a park or the woods, consider purchasing a beautiful bouquet of flowers and allowing that to be your sacred text speaking to you of the holy in creation.

For Reflection

Where are your favorite places to be out in creation? The beach, the mountains, a lake, a grassy plain, the desert, a rushing waterfall?

How have the landscapes of your life shaped your spiritual journey?

Have you had moments when you could hear the hymn nature was singing?

How has nature been a teacher for you?

THE SACRED STORIES OF OUR LIVES

*All beings / are words of God, /
His music, His / art.
Sacred books we are, for the infinite camps /
in our / souls.*

—Meister Eckhart

*Like the Hebrew alphabet, the alphabet of grace has
no vowels, and in that sense [God's] words to us are
always veiled, subtle, cryptic, so that it is left to us to
delve their meaning, to fill in the vowels, for ourselves by means of all the faith and imagination we
can muster. God speaks to us in such a way. Out of
the shadowy street comes a cry for help. We must
learn to listen to the cock-crows and hammering and
tick-tock of our lives for the holy and elusive word
that is spoken to us out of their depths.*

—Frederick Buechner, The Alphabet of Grace

In this final chapter, we will explore our lives as a source of sacred
texts and stories for *lectio divina*. This includes our life experience, dreams, and bodies, as well as the stories of others.
Ultimately, the practice of *lectio* invites us to consider how we

might read each moment as shimmering with Sacred Presence. The German poet Rainer Maria Rilke once suggested that if the tasks of our days seem unrewarding, we should not blame them but ourselves for failing to be present and fully aware of the grace hidden there. If, as Meister Eckhart writes, we are each words of God, sacred books, then each page from our lives reveals something of the Holy. We don't often see it because it is so challenging. We live with dulled vision, so we only see life's surfaces—the demands and anxieties and struggles of daily living—or we numb ourselves to the pain with distractions, deafening our ears to the call to rest in silence and listen.

In the eighteenth century a form of Jewish mysticism emerged called Hasidism, which taught that because God is everywhere and in everything, the possibility of encountering the Holy is offered in each moment. Every ordinary action such as work or eating has the spark of holiness waiting to be revealed. In the Hasidic worldview, the "life task of the Jew was to make that potential actual. This was done not by saying special prayers or doing things in a special Jewish way, but by being acutely aware of the potential in every moment."[1] The rituals and blessings of Jewish life are not meant to be practiced for their own sake, but for the sake of deepening awareness.

This Hasidic worldview is very similar to the monastic path. Praying the hours and reading Scripture are not ends in themselves, but doorways to a widened capacity for awareness that God dwells in each moment. What *lectio divina* offers to us is a method and practice for cultivating this awareness in all aspects of our lives.

We constantly tell the stories of our lives. Sometimes the story we tell, however, keeps us stuck in certain patterns of expectation. We can outgrow who we understand ourselves to be. For example, I spent many years training as an academic. Graduate work demands a certain writing style and way of thinking about things. When I finished my PhD, I began to look for a teaching position at a university even though I wasn't entirely sure it was what I wanted; I had been immersed in academic life for so long that it was hard to let go of that story of myself. My two great loves had always been writing and creating sacred space for others. Slowly I began to shift my perspective and saw how my academic training gave me a strong footing, but it was only a part of who I am. To my great delight, I began to pursue a life as an author and a teacher of spiritual practice. It was through my commitment to the practice of *lectio divina* that I began to remember all the parts of who I am and what brings me joy. In my prayer the images that kept shimmering were the contemplative peace I find through hours spent crafting the written word or the satisfaction of creating a safe space for others to explore their buried dreams and hidden inner landscapes.

Stories can be empowering, but also limiting. The invitation to pray with our lives is not about reaffirming what we already know about ourselves, but entering into prayer in an open-hearted way to receive the grace and new vision offered to us. We pray with our lives as sacred texts to reveal new places of freedom, giving us invitations to new ways of understanding ourselves and the ways God is moving through our stories.

Invitation to Practice: *Lectio* with Life Experience

> If there is any path at all on which I can approach You, it must lead through the very middle of my ordinary daily life. If You have given me no single place to which I can flee and be sure of finding You, then I must be able to find You in every place in each and every thing I do. In Your love all the diffusion of the day's chores comes home again to the evening of Your unity, which is eternal life.
>
> —Karl Rahner, Meditations and Prayers

The Jesuit theologian Karl Rahner described all moments and experiences as potentially revelatory. As he writes, we can only approach the Holy One through the path of ordinary daily life. It is this path that I am suggesting for bringing the practice of *lectio divina* to life experience. In addition to praying with the moments of our day, we might also consider the body a sacred text, dreams as a place of revelation, and the daily newspaper as a way to enter into solidarity with the suffering of others.

Settling and Shimmering

Begin your time of prayer by deciding which life experience you want to focus on. You might choose to pray with the past twenty-four hours, or with the past week or month or season. If you have just been through an experience like a pilgrimage or retreat, allow that to be the text. To begin, I suggest praying with the past day, and then you can move through this same experience with different focuses.

Allow some time to settle into your chair and sink into your body. Become aware of your breathing, gently deepening it. As you inhale, imagine the breath of God filling not just your body but also the whole of your life with enlivening energy. As you exhale, imagine letting go of whatever keeps you from being fully present to your life.

Allow your breath to carry your awareness down to your heart center. Rest in this space for a few moments, perhaps resting your hand over your heart and relishing the rhythm of your heartbeat, which sustains your life.

Savoring and Stirring

Begin to "read" your experience. In your imagination, walk through this past day, noticing where your attention is being drawn, welcoming in whatever memories or feelings arise. Move through the day in an openhearted and spacious way, and notice if there is a particular moment that wants some more attention. Listen for how your heart is being led. Make room within you to allow this moment to unfold in your imagination. Savor the sense experience of it. What do you remember of sight, smell, taste, touch, and sound? Are there images, colors, or symbols rising up into your awareness? Be present to the feelings that are being stirred and welcome them in.

Summoning and Serving

Begin to shift your awareness and become open to the ways God was present to you in this experience. Do you sense how you are being called in your life to respond to this moment? What action or awareness is emerging from your reflection on this time?

Slowing and Stilling

Gently release everything that has been stirring in you. Connect to your breath again and allow the rhythm of your breath to fill you with peace, letting go of words and images so you can rest fully into a few moments of contemplative presence. Give yourself some time simply to be, remembering that your life is about more than the sum of your experiences and what you do in the world. Then release even this awareness and come to a place of deep stillness.

When you are ready to complete this time of prayer, allow your breath to bring your awareness gently back to the outer space of your room. Take some time to journal about what emerged in your prayer experience, writing about any moment that called for more attention.

Further Possibilities for Practice

When it comes to our life story and experience, there are a wide variety of possible texts. Every action has the potential for deeper awareness and presence. Here are three more suggestions for ways to bring *lectio divina* into your life in a more integrated way.

Praying *Lectio* with the Body

You can practice *lectio divina* with your body as a sacred text. Enter into the meditation I have just described, but instead of moving through a day in your imagination, scan through your body. Begin with your feet and slowly move your awareness through your legs, hips, groin, back, stomach, shoulders, arms, fingers, neck, head, and face. Notice if there is one place in your body needing more attention. Be present to this place, bringing your breath there, softening into it, opening to memories and feelings.

If this form of practice appeals to you, I highly recommend *Broken Body, Healing Spirit: Lectio Divina and Living with Illness* by Mary Earle.

Praying *Lectio* with Dreams

Lectio divina can also be a powerful way to pray with our dreams as a sacred text. Dreams are another form of God's communication to us in intuitive and symbolic ways, and the scriptures are filled with stories of significant dreams that shape the dreamer's action in the world. When you awaken from a dream, write it down in present tense and try to recall as many images and feelings as you can remember. Enter into prayer with the dream as a sacred text. You can either read your summary of the experience or close your eyes and try to re-enter the dream's energy.

If you are not in the habit of recording your dreams, consider keeping pen and paper by your bed and when you wake up in the morning allow some time to connect with the dreams stirring in your consciousness. Write the dream in present tense, date it, and give it a title. Remember that dreams speak in a nonlinear way, so it might not make logical sense.

Then bring the four movements of *lectio divina* to the dream. Settle in and connect with your breath, moving your awareness to your heart. Read through the dream with heart-centered awareness and listen for an image or a phrase that is shimmering for you. Allow some space for it to unfold, savoring the images that emerge. Pay attention to the feelings stirred by this dream image. Listen for the invitation arising from your prayer. Then sit in silence, offering gratitude for a God who speaks to us even in our sleep.

Praying *Lectio* with the Newspaper

> *Christ has no body now but yours,*
> *No hands, no feet on earth but yours.*
> *Yours are the eyes through which He looks*
> *compassion on this world.*
> *Christ has no body now on earth but yours.*
> —Teresa of Avila

The text of the daily newspaper can be a powerful place from which to pray. The stories we read of tragedy and crisis, as well as reconciliation and hope, offer us sacred moments in which to enter into solidarity with others. Sometimes we can feel overwhelmed by what the news brings each day, but the practice of *lectio divina* can help us respond from a heart-centered place.

Praying *lectio divina* with a story that is calling to your heart can give you a meaningful way to be with this experience and listen for your own calling in response. Read slowly through St. Teresa's meditation offered above and, instead of praying with the events of your day, select a small section of a news story to be your text for prayer.

Settle into your body and draw your breath deeply into your belly. Become fully present to this moment. Bring your awareness to your heart.

Slowly read a portion of the news story. Listen for the word or phrase shimmering. Repeat it gently to yourself.

Open your heart even wider and allow the word or phrase to unfold within you, making space for the images, memories, and feelings that stir in response.

Ask if there is some awareness or action you are being called to out of this time of prayer. Notice how your heart wants to respond.

Allow some time for silence to simply rest into the gift of being.

For Reflection

What would it mean for you to consider your life story a sacred text? How might the moments of joy and sorrow become even more meaningful?

When the troubles of the world feel overwhelming, how might bringing your *lectio divina* practice to praying with these stories in the news help ground and center you?

If you were to consider your body a sacred text, how might you listen differently to its longings?

A F T E R W O R D

THE DIVINE PRESENCE
IS EVERYWHERE

But as we progress in this way of life and in faith,
we shall run on the path of God's commandments,
our hearts overflowing with the inexpressible delight
of love.

—*Rule of Benedict, Prologue: 49*

The purpose of contemplative practice is cultivation of freedom and compassion. As we grow in inner freedom, we become less caught up in the demands of life. We begin to let go of our compulsions to grow ever busier. As we learn to welcome in the full spectrum of our own emotional landscape with gentleness and compassion, the more we grow in our capacity to offer that grace to others. As we draw closer to the cave of our hearts, where we meet God within our very being, we begin to recognize this luminosity in others.

Thomas Merton writes of such an epiphany on the street corner of 4th and Walnut in Louisville, Kentucky:

I was suddenly overwhelmed with the realization that I loved all those people, that they were mine and I theirs, that we could not be alien to one another even though we were total strangers. It was like waking from a dream of separateness ... Then it was as if I suddenly saw the secret beauty of their hearts, the depths of their hearts where neither sin nor desire nor self-knowledge can reach, the core of their reality, the person that each one is in God's eyes. If only they could all see themselves as they really are. If only we could see each other that way all the time. There would be no more war, no more hatred, no more cruelty, no more greed.[1]

We practice the way of life that Merton describes on behalf of a commitment to greater peace. As we learn to strengthen our inner witness and cultivate our capacity for calm, nonanxious presence in the midst of life's struggles, we begin to offer that peaceful, centered presence to the world. We no longer contribute to the world's growing anxiety and mistrust of one another. Our prayer shapes our life; our life shapes our prayer. There is a continuous dialectic, a mutual exchange of hearts.

ALWAYS WE BEGIN AGAIN

It is wise to hold all of these worthy goals with humility. Benedict describes his rule of life as a "little Rule for beginners," and because we are human we will continue to stray from the path we most deeply long for. Life will intervene and throw us off track. We will need to bring ourselves back again and again to the practice.

In *Wherever You Go, There You Are*, Jon Kabat-Zinn writes that doing yoga and not doing yoga are the same. What he means is that sometimes when we return to our practice after having left it for several days (or weeks, months, years) we often have a deeper appreciation for what we have lost than if we had not strayed. "Always we begin again" are perhaps the four most important words to me in Benedict's rule, and I repeat them often to my students in contemplative practice. Beginning again is essential. We fall away, we lose our will to persevere for so many reasons. The problem is not with the waning of our inner fire and perseverance, but with not returning again at all. When we realize we have not meditated in days, and so our minds have become hard with judgment and self-criticism, we find ourselves even further from the peace we might experience than if we had simply returned to practice without anxiety.

Kabat-Zinn also asks, "Can you see that not practicing is an arduous practice?" What he means is that we each have a life practice, although it may not be conscious or intentional. When we cultivate compassion and peace in ourselves through *lectio divina*, meditation, chanting, yoga, or any number of possible practices, it spills over into the rest of our lives. When we have no intentional practice, we may move through life full of anxiety and resentment, with no way to hold grief and the struggles of life. To have no practice becomes the most arduous kind of practice. When we remember this, returning to our practice comes with greater ease because we recognize how much harder life is without it.

DOES GOD REALLY SPEAK?

The underlying assumption of *lectio divina* is that the whole world is, in fact, a text of sacred revelation. All experience has the potential to be revelatory, and God is singing one unending song, seducing each of our hearts, so the call is to listen, to attune ourselves to the words God utters into the world. As we have discovered in this book, the way God speaks is elusive and often mysterious, for God's voice is the language of dreams and landscapes, of art and music, of dancing and poetry. It does not lend itself easily to a world conditioned to sound bites. In moments of simple kindness and compassion, in the quiet knowing of my heart's desires, in the profound impulse toward life in every moment, even in my weeping, which witnesses to my capacity for great love, I don't ask whether God is speaking. I ask whether there can be any place void of this sacred song.

As we practice *lectio divina*, its rhythm works its way into our hearts. We may find that we are spontaneously noticing a shimmering moment during the day, or that when our imaginations want to widen and unfold we allow them space, or we listen more closely to the quiet nudgings of the heart.

If we show up day after day to the gifts of *lectio divina*, our lives slowly become woven with the symbols and stories we encounter in the sacred texts with which we pray. Perhaps more than anything else, we discover our hearts are more attuned to the movements of the Sacred in each moment. We no longer worry about whether we get the steps right and we surrender ourselves into the natural grace and rhythm of our heart's deepest longings.

ACKNOWLEDGMENTS

My heart is overflowing with gratitude for:

My husband, John, who offered much encouragement, love, and many play dates as I worked on this material.

My students who have participated in the many classes and retreats I have led on *lectio divina*. Their whole-hearted seeking, passionate engagement, and thoughtful questions have helped deepen my own understanding of the movements of this beautiful form of prayer.

Emily Wichland of SkyLight Paths Publishing for requesting this book and being such a responsive and enthusiastic supporter of this work.

Cynthia Shattuck for her very fine editing.

R E T R E A T   E X P E R I E N C E

When I enter into the silence and spaciousness of retreat time, I hear the quiet inner voices that get drowned out in the rush of daily life. I have had life-changing moments on retreat, and encountered longings that carried me over new thresholds. I have been transformed in my willingness to meet myself. On retreat I can walk for hours among trees, I can gaze upon the unfolding of wave after wave. I sleep when I feel tired, I write pages and pages from a heart that begins to see things widely again. Daily life can narrow my vision and tighten my gaze. Retreat invites expansion, the pondering of horizons, the dancing on edges.

Retreats come in many shapes and sizes. Sometimes all that is necessary is an hour with the phone and computer turned off, a cup of tea, a journal and pen, and some silence to begin to reconnect with the heart. Consider beginning with a one-day retreat.

SUGGESTED SOLO DAY RETREAT FORMAT

Here is a suggested format for a daylong retreat experience of *lectio divina*. Adapt the time frame to your needs; this is only a loose structure for guidance.

PREPARING FOR YOUR RETREAT TIME

If possible, go away to another space where you will have as little distraction as possible. I work from home and so sometimes it can be challenging for me to use my house as retreat space; it seems there is always work waiting for me there. But it can work—sometimes it is simply a matter of retreating to a special room or area designated for this time, and turning off the phone and computer. Schedule your retreat time in and hold it sacred. If necessary, let family and friends know that you are taking some time for solitude and would appreciate their respecting that commitment unless there is an emergency.

SUPPLIES

Bring a passage (Scripture, poetry, an image, a piece of music) selected for prayer, a journal, a pen, a small meal, a book of prayers or poems, some colored markers, paper, magazines for collage images, scissors, and glue sticks.

9–10:30 A.M.

Begin your day with a prayer or blessing for this time. If you haven't already, write a blessing you can read as you begin each prayer time. In Chapter Three there is a suggested blessing with movements. Name your intention for the day, which isn't so much an expectation as a gentle cue to yourself as to why you are making this commitment.

This first part of the morning is dedicated to the first movement of *lectio*. Allow some time for preparation and connecting with your body, breath, and heart. Then turn to your passage for prayer, perhaps one from this book that really sparked your imagination, or ask a spiritual director if there is one he or she would recommend in light of your life stage right now. Allow as much time as you need to settle on the word or phrase shimmering for you, and then allow the rest of the time to simply explore the word or phrase through some of the suggestions in Chapter Five: learn it by heart, repeat it as a mantra, take some colored pens and paper and write it over and over again in an act of visual meditation.

After some time immersed in the first movement, shift to the second movement.

10:30 A.M.—12:00 P.M.

Bring the word or phrase out on a long walk. As you put one foot in front of the other, notice the deepening of your breath, the beating of your heart. Make space to allow your mind and heart to make connections to images, memories, feelings. Perhaps something in nature will resonate with your word or phrase and allow it to continue to unfold.

You might experiment with chanting your word aloud as you walk.

12:00—1:00 P.M.

Return to your retreat space and prepare a meal slowly and with great care. Eat mindfully, allowing each flavor to linger in your mouth. Give gratitude for the way this food nourishes and sustains your work in the world.

1:00—3:00 P.M.

Spend some time reflecting on the invitation in your life right now emerging from your engagement with the text. This is a wonderful time for collage, poetry writing, or journaling. Allow art to be the container for your sacred call emerging.

3:00—3:30 P.M.

Close the day with some extended time in silence, simply basking in the grace of stillness. Offer a prayer of gratitude, naming the gifts of the day and what you bring back to your daily life.

APPENDIX 2

LECTIO DIVINA AS A SMALL GROUP EXPERIENCE

While *lectio divina* has traditionally been a solitary practice, in recent years a group form of *lectio* has become popular and widely practiced. This can be a beautiful way to share your experience of a sacred text with others and break open a deepened experience of prayer in community.

This form of *lectio* works best in a group of four to six people. It can be expanded for up to twelve people but there will be less intimacy and time for sharing. For each gathering it is important to have someone designated as the leader who will create the space, select the sacred text, and guide the process. In my Benedictine oblate community we regularly practice *lectio divina* together and rotate leadership of the experience.

Below is a sample format for leading a group *lectio* session. Essentially, the leader reads the sacred text aloud and guides the reflection on each of the movements. There are periods of silence after each reading and then an opportunity for participants to each share the fruits of a particular movement. It can be profound to hear the many ways the same text is working on the hearts of others and it often leads to insightful heart-centered conversation around the places we are seeking more support in life.

I have also led group *lectio divina* practices for Advent and Lent. For these I have created space after our prayer for art experiences with the sacred texts (usually one from the Sunday readings). Then there is time at the end to share what emerged in the time of creative expression.

OVERVIEW OF THE PROCESS

SUPPLIES
Participants bring a journal and pen. Facilitator brings a passage of sacred text for *lectio divina*, an opening prayer, candle, matches, chime, clock, box of tissues, and any other symbols for the altar space that feel meaningful.

SUGGESTED SCHEDULE
Ninety minutes total. If you want to include more time for conversation or for art-making consider extending the time to two hours.

(5 minutes) **Opening Prayer**
Offer a simple reading or poem to set the theme or invite participants into a few moments of silence to gather themselves and become present.

(20 minutes) **Checking In**
Each session might begin with a brief check-in time for participants to share how they are feeling as they come to the gathering. This could be as simple as naming whether they are tired, energized, distracted, sad, and so forth, or it could involve sharing a short story about a significant recent event in their lives. If you are participating in a series, the first week invite participants to share their hopes and longings and any challenges they anticipate.

Divide the 20 minutes between the number of participants (for example, with five participants, each person has about 4 minutes). The facilitator can then keep track of time and offer a gentle visual cue if someone is reaching the end of his or her time. After each person speaks, invite just a moment of silence to honor his or her story, and then ring the chime to indicate the next person's turn.

(30 minutes)   **Group *Lectio Divina***
The facilitator leads the group in an experience of group *lectio divina* that includes verbal sharing after each movement. See below for guidelines. Select the passage from the Sunday readings or choose a specific theme you wish to explore.

(10 minutes)   **Silent Reflection and Journaling**
Allow some time for silent reflection on the *lectio divina* experience and journaling about what words, images, memories, and invitations emerged during prayer.

(20 minutes)   **Closing Sharing—Becoming God's Word in the World**
As you close, take a few moments each to share the fruits of this prayer time. Ask participants to share their thoughts on their commitment for the next session and how it rises from this prayer experience.

(5 minutes)   **Closing Prayer**
Enter into some shared silence or engage in a group prayer and blessing.

SUGGESTIONS FOR LEADING GROUP *LECTIO DIVINA*

Praying *lectio divina* in a group setting can be a powerful way to experience the unique impact a particular text has on different peoples' lives. Hearing what is moving in other participants in response to the text as the prayer unfolds can allow us to see things we hadn't seen before.

Below is a suggested script for leading a group *lectio* prayer session. Feel free to use whatever words make sense for you. You may also want to have different participants read the selected scriptural text each time to hear it from different voices.

Remind participants that there will be moments to share what is stirring in them, and during this time of sharing there should be no cross-talk or conversation. This is a time to just be present to one another. You can allow time following the prayer experience for dialogue.

PREPARATION

Invite the participants to take some time to become fully present to the moment:

> Close your eyes and shift your body so you feel comfortable. Become conscious of your breathing.
>
> As you inhale, breathe in the life-giving breath of the Holy. As you exhale, release and surrender into this moment, setting aside your distractions and worries. Take a few moments to be present to this rhythm within you. Gently allow your breath to draw your awareness from your head down to your heart and receive the gift of sacred scriptures with the ear of your heart.

SETTLING AND SHIMMERING

Invite participants to listen for a word or phrase that is calling to them right now.

> In your initial encounter with the passage listen for a word or phrase that shimmers. This is the word or phrase that beckons you, addresses you, unnerves you, disturbs you, stirs you, or seems especially ripe with meaning. I am going to read the passage twice.

Read the selected passage aloud, twice, slowly (or ask two participants to each read the passage through once).

> Identify the word or phrase that shimmers for you and repeat that word or phrase to yourself in the silence.

Allow about a minute of silence and then invite participants to share their word or phrase with the group if they so desire. After everyone who wants to share has done so, move to the next step.

SAVORING AND STIRRING

I am going to read the passage again. In the silence that follows, gently repeat the word or phrase to yourself, allowing it to unfold in your imagination. Savor the images that rise up. Notice the memories and feelings that stir in you in response. Make space within your heart to welcome these in.

Read the passage again (or have another participant read it).

Allow another minute or more of silence and then invite participants to share a feeling, a memory, or an image that is moving in them. After everyone who wants to has shared, move to the next step.

SUMMONING AND SERVING

I am going to read the passage one more time. In the silence that follows, pay attention to the way the word, image, feeling, or memory connects with your life right now in this moment. What kind of awareness or action might God be inviting you to in light of this? Is God calling you to do something in response to your prayer? Notice how your heart wants to respond to the ways God has been speaking in this time of prayer.

Read the Scripture passage again (or have another participant read it).

Allow 2 to 3 minutes of silence, and then invite participants to share any invitation they sense from this time of prayer. After everyone who wants to has shared move to the next step.

SLOWING AND STILLING

Invite participants into a time of silent contemplation.

> Release all of the words and images that have been moving in you and take a few moments to simply rest in the presence of God.

Allow another 2 to 3 minutes of silence.

> Allow your heart to fill with gratitude for whatever has been revealed in this time. Connect again to the rhythm of your breath, breathing in the life-giving breath of Spirit, exhaling and releasing into this moment of time. Slowly and gently allow your breath to carry your awareness from your internal space back to this room.

If you have a chime, ring it three times slowly, inviting participants to allow the sound to carry them back to the group.

Move from the *lectio divina* experience into a time of silent reflection, inviting participants to take about 10 minutes to journal what they experienced. Ring the chime again when there is about a minute left and then gather back together for sharing.

CONVERSATION

Allow some time to move into prayerful conversation that emerges from the *lectio* experience.

Close your time together by reading a poem or prayer or offering spontaneous blessing as you each move back out into the world.

A P P E N D I X   3

M A N D A L A

NOTES

CHAPTER 1
SACRED READING:
LISTENING FOR A SACRED WORD

1. Richard McCambly, www.lectio-divina.org.
2. Carl J. Arico, *A Taste of Silence* (New York: Continuum, 1999), 103.
3. Mariano Magrassi, *Praying the Bible: Introduction to Lectio Divina* (Collegeville, MN: Liturgical Press, 1998), 22.
4. Lex Hixon, *The Heart of the Qur'an* (Wheaton, IL: Theosophical Publishing House, 1988), 4–5.
5. Jean-Yves Leloup, *Being Still: Reflections on an Ancient Mystical Tradition* (Mahwah, NJ: Paulist Press, 2003), 89.
6. Leloup, *Being Still*, 86.
7. Magrassi, *Praying the Bible*, 38.
8. Quoted by Bede Griffiths in *Universal Wisdom: A Journey through the Sacred Wisdom of the World* (New York: HarperCollins, 1994), 299.

CHAPTER 2
AT THE HEART OF *LECTIO DIVINA*:
BENEDICTINE SPIRITUALITY AND
HEART-CENTERED PRAYER

1. Kallistos Ware, "How Do We Enter the Heart?" in James Cutsinger, ed., *Paths to the Heart: Sufism and the Christian East* (Bloomington, IN: World Wisdom, 2004), 9.
2. Seyyed Hossein Nasr, "The Heart of the Faithful Is the Throne of the All-Merciful," in Cutsinger, *Paths to the Heart*, 37.
3. Norvene Vest, *Gathered in the Word: Praying the Scripture in Small Groups* (Nashville, TN: Upper Room, 1998), 34–35.
4. Cutsinger, *Paths to the Heart*, 7.

5. Rabindranath Tagore, *The Heart of God*, ed. Herbert H. Vetter (North Clarendon, VT: Tuttle, 2004), 67.

CHAPTER 3
THE ROLE OF SPIRITUAL PRACTICE:
CULTIVATING WAYS OF BEING IN THE WORLD

1. Don Saliers, *Worship and Spirituality* (Louisville, KY: Westminster John Knox, 1984), 31.

2. Cyprian Consiglio, *Prayer in the Cave of the Heart: The Universal Call to Contemplation* (Collegeville, MN: Liturgical Press, 2010), 12.

3. Esther de Waal, *Seeking God: The Way of St. Benedict* (Collegeville, MN: Liturgical Press, 2001), 65.

4. Maria Lichtmann, *The Teacher's Way: Teaching and the Contemplative Life* (Mahwah, NJ: Paulist Press, 2005), 25–26.

5. Eugene Peterson, *Eat This Book: A Conversation in the Art of Spiritual Reading* (Grand Rapids, MI: Eerdmans, 2009), 68.

6. Thomas Merton, *New Seeds of Contemplation* (New York: New Directions, 2007), 296–7.

7. Michael Casey, *Sacred Reading: The Ancient Art of Lectio Divina* (Liguori, MO: Liguori Publications, 1996), 6.

8. Mu Soeng, *The Diamond Sutra: Transforming the Way We See the World* (Boston: Wisdom Publications, 2000), 145.

CHAPTER 4
"GIVE ME A WORD":
CHOOSING TEXTS FOR *LECTIO DIVINA*

1. *The Rule of St. Benedict* (Collegeville, MN: Liturgical Press, 1982), 73:2–6.

2. Rudolf Otto, *The Idea of the Holy*, trans. John Harvey (Oxford: Oxford University Press, 1958), 12.

3. See www.usccb.org/nab for the United States Conference of Catholic Bishops site with a list of the daily readings. See lectionary.library.vanderbilt.edu for the Revised Common Lectionary readings at the Vanderbilt Divinity Library website.

4. Casey, *Sacred Reading*, 24.

5. Hafiz, *The Gift*, trans. Daniel Ladinsky (New York: Penguin, 1999), 160.

6. Annie Dillard, *Holy the Firm* (New York: Harper & Row, 1977), 11–12.

CHAPTER 5
LISTENING FOR GOD'S VOICE:
LECTIO'S CALL TO AWAKEN TO THE DIVINE

1. www.hir.org/a_weekly_gallery/8.16.02-weekly.html.

2. Kay Lindahl, *The Sacred Art of Listening: Forty Reflections for Cultivating a Spiritual Practice* (Woodstock, VT: Skylight Paths, 2002), 11.

3. Consiglio, *Prayer in the Cave of the Heart*, 35.

4. Margaret McGee, *Haiku: A Spiritual Practice in Three Lines* (Woodstock, VT: Skylight Paths, 2009), 91.

CHAPTER 6
SAVORING SACRED TEXT:
MEDITATIO'S WELCOMING WITH ALL SENSES

1. Nanette Sawyer, *Hospitality: The Sacred Art: Discovering the Hidden Spiritual Power of Invitation and Welcome* (Woodstock, VT: SkyLight Paths, 2008), 4–5.

2. Thich Nhat Hanh, "Seeding the Unconscious: New Views on Buddhism and Psychotherapy," *Common Boundary* (Nov/Dec, 1989), 19.

3. Walter Brueggemann, *The Prophetic Imagination* (Minneapolis, MN: Fortress Press, 2001), 11, 3.

CHAPTER 7
SUMMONING YOUR TRUE SELF:
HEARING *ORATIO*'S CALL OF THE SPIRIT

1. Roberta Bondi, *To Pray and to Love* (Minneapolis, MN: Augsburg Fortress, 1991), 101.

2. Leloup, *Being Still*, 14–15.

3. Michael Casey, OCS, *A Guide to Living in the Truth* (Liguori, MO: Liguori Publications, 2001), 5.

4. Leloup, *Being Still*, 26.

5. Casey, *Sacred Reading*, 29.

6. Casey, *Sacred Reading*, 29–30.

7. John Chryssavgis, *In the Heart of the Desert: The Spirituality of the Desert Fathers and Mothers* (Bloomington, IN: World Wisdom, 2008), 468.

8. Rule of Benedict, 3.

9. De Waal, *Seeking God*, 42–43.

10. Norvene Vest, *Gathered in the Word* (Nashville, TN: Upper Room, 1998), 42.

CHAPTER 8
THE GIFT OF BEING:
RESTING *CONTEMPLATIO*'S STILLNESS
AND SILENCE

1. Martin Laird, *Into the Silent Land: A Guide to the Christian Practice of Contemplation* (New York: Oxford University Press, 2006), 116.

2. A. J. V. Chandrakanthan, "The Silence of Buddha and His Contemplation of the Truth," *Spirituality Today* 40:2, 145–156.

3. Kallistos Ware, *The Power of the Name, The Jesus Prayer in Orthodox Spirituality* (New York: Oxford, 1991), 1.

4. Thomas Merton, *The Sign of Jonas* (Orlando, FL: Harcourt, 1981), 343.

5. Kahlil Gibran, letter to Mary Haskell, March 1, 1918.

CHAPTER 9
VISIO DIVINA:
PRAYING WITH IMAGES

1. Heather Williams Durka, "Icon of Theotokos," www.iconsandsacredimages.com.

2. Available at www.stacywills.com.

CHAPTER 10
AUDIO DIVINA:
PRAYING WITH SOUND

1. Rohit Mehta, *The Call of the Upanishads* (New Delhi: Motilal Banarsidass, 1999), 147.

CHAPTER 11
NATURE AS SACRED TEXT

1. Quoted in Leloup, *Being Still*, 83–84.
2. Leloup, *Being Still*, 2.
3. Leloup, *Being Still*, 12.
4. Ajahn Chah, *Forest Sangha Newsletter*.

CHAPTER 12
THE SACRED STORIES OF OUR LIVES

1. Michael Strassfeld, *A Book of Life: Embracing Judaism as Spiritual Practice* (Woodstock, VT: Jewish Lights, 2006), xiv.

AFTERWORD:
THE DIVINE PRESENCE IS EVERYWHERE

1. Thomas Merton, *Conjectures of a Guilty Bystander* (Garden City, NY: Doubleday, 1968), 156.

SUGGESTED RESOURCES

LECTIO DIVINA AND CONTEMPLATIVE PRAYER

Arico, Carl J. *A Taste of Silence: A Guide to the Fundamentals of Centering Prayer.* New York: Continuum, 1999.

Bourgeault, Cynthia. *Centering Prayer and Inner Awakening.* Boston: Cowley Publications, 2004.

_____. *The Wisdom Way of Knowing.* San Francisco: Jossey-Bass, 2003.

Casey, Michael. *Sacred Reading: The Ancient Art of Lectio Divina.* Ligouri, MO: Liguori Publications, 1996.

Chittister, Joan. *The Rule of Saint Benedict: Insight for the Ages.* New York: Crossroads, 2002.

Chryssavgis, John. *In the Heart of the Desert: The Spirituality of the Desert Fathers and Mothers.* Bloomington, IN: World Wisdom, 2008.

Consiglio, Cyprian, OSB. *Prayer in the Cave of the Heart: The Universal Call to Contemplation.* Collegeville, MN: Liturgical Press, 2010.

de Waal, Esther. *Seeking God: The Way of St. Benedict.* Collegeville, MN: Liturgical Press, 2001.

Earle, Mary. *Broken Body, Healing Spirit: Lectio Divina and Living with Illness.* Harrisburg, PA: Morehouse Publishing, 2003.

Fry, Timothy, OSB, ed. *The Rule of St. Benedict.* Collegeville, MN: Liturgical Press, 1981.

Funk, Mary Margaret. *Lectio Matters: Before the Burning Bush.* New York: Continuum, 2010.

Guigo II. *Ladder of Monks.* Kalamazoo, MI: Cistercian Publications, 1981.

Laird, Martin, *Into the Silent Land: A Guide to the Christian Practice of Contemplation.* New York: Oxford University Press, 2006.

Leloup, Jean-Yves. *Being Still: Reflections on an Ancient Mystical Tradition.* Mahwah, NJ: Paulist Press, 2003.

Lichtmann, Maria. *The Teacher's Way: Teaching and the Contemplative Life*. Mahwah, NJ: Paulist Press, 2005.

Magrassi, Mariano. *Praying the Bible: Introduction to* Lectio Divina. Collegeville, MN: Liturgical Press, 1998.

Merton, Thomas. *Conjectures of a Guilty Bystander*. Garden City, NY: Doubleday, 1968.

_____. *New Seeds of Contemplation*. New York: New Directions, 2007.

Nouwen, Henri. *The Way of the Heart*. New York: Ballantine Books, 2003.

Paintner, Christine Valters, and Lucy Wynkoop, OSB. Lectio Divina: *Contemplative Awakening and Awareness*. Mahwah, NJ: Paulist Press, 2008.

Peterson, Eugene. *Eat This Book: A Conversation in the Art of Spiritual Reading*. Grand Rapids, MI: William B. Eerdmans, 2009.

Smith, Cyprian, OSB. *The Path of Life*. Leominster, UK: Gracewing Publishing, 1995.

Smith, Martin L.. *The Word Is Very Near You: A Guide to Praying with Scripture*. Boston: Cowley Publications, 1989.

Studzinski, Raymond. *Reading to Live: The Evolving Practice of Lectio Divina*. Kalamazoo, MI: Cistercian Publications, 2009.

Vest, Norvene. *Friend of the Soul: A Benedictine Spirituality of Work*. Boston: Cowley Publications, 1997.

_____. *Gathered in the Word: Praying the Scripture in Small Groups*. Nashville, TN: Upper Room, 1998.

Vivian, Tom, ed. *Becoming Fire: Through the Year with the Desert Fathers and Mothers*. Kalamazoo, MI: Cistercian Publications, 2008.

OTHER RESOURCES

Bass, Dorothy, and Craig Dykstra. *Practicing Our Faith: A Way of Life for a Searching People*. San Francisco: Jossey-Bass, 2010.

Brueggemann, Walter. *The Prophetic Imagination*. Minneapolis, MN: Fortress Press, 2001.

Casey, Michael. *A Guide to Living in the Truth: St. Benedict's Teaching on Humility*. Liguori, MO: Ligouri Publications, 2001.

Cutsinger, James, ed. *Paths to the Heart: Sufism and the Christian East*. Bloomington, IN: World Wisdom, 2002.

Griffiths, Bede. *Universal Wisdom: A Journey through the Sacred Wisdom of the World*. San Francisco: HarperCollins, 1994.

Hixon, Lex. *The Heart of the Qur'an*. Wheaton, IL: Theosophical Publishing House, 2003.

Kabat-Zinn, Jon. *Wherever You Go, There You Are*. New York: Hyperion, 2005.

McGee, Margaret. *Haiku: A Spiritual Practice in Three Lines*. Woodstock, VT: SkyLight Paths, 2009.

Mehta, Rohit. *The Call of the Upanishads*. New Delhi: Motilal Banarsidass, 1990.

Saliers, Don. *Worship and Spirituality*. Nitro, WV: Order of St. Luke Publications, 1998.

Strassfeld, Michael. *A Book of Life: Embracing Judaism as a Spiritual Practice*. Woodstock, VT: Jewish Lights, 2006.

Rahner, Karl. *Meditations and Prayers*. New York: Seabury Press, 1980.

THE WORLD'S SACRED SCRIPTURES
CHRISTIAN SCRIPTURE

The Message: A contemporary translation by theologian Eugene Peterson.

New American Bible: The official translation of the United States Conference of Catholic Bishops for use in the lectionary readings at Mass.

New Jerusalem Bible: A Roman Catholic translation.

New Revised Standard Version: A translation by the National Council of Churches, an ecumenical Christian group.

HEBREW BIBLE

Jewish Publication Society's *Tanakh*: The primary translation for all forms of English-speaking Judaism outside of Orthodox Judaism.

Tanach: The Stone Edition (Mesorah Publications): Popular in the Orthodox Jewish community, this volume includes introductions to each book and a running commentary based on classic rabbinic interpretation.

QUR'AN

The Holy Qur'an (Syed V. Mir Ahmed 'Ali): This translation has become the standard Shi'ite translation.

The Holy Qur'an: Translation and Commentary (Abdullah Yusuf 'Ali): From its first appearance in 1934 until very recently, this was the most popular English version among Muslims.

The Koran Interpreted (Arthur Arberry): This 1955 translation acknowledged the orthodox Muslim view that the Qu'ran cannot be translated, but only interpreted.

Judaism / Christianity / Islam / Interfaith

Christians & Jews—Faith to Faith: Tragic History, Promising Present, Fragile Future *by Rabbi James Rudin*
A probing examination of Christian-Jewish relations that looks at the major issues facing both faith communities. 6 x 9, 288 pp, HC, 978-1-58023-432-0 **$24.99***

Getting to the Heart of Interfaith
The Eye-Opening, Hope-Filled Friendship of a Pastor, a Rabbi and a Sheikh
by Pastor Don Mackenzie, Rabbi Ted Falcon and Imam Jamal Rahman
Offers many insights and encouragements for individuals and groups who want to tap into the promise of interfaith dialogue. 6 x 9, 192 pp, Quality PB, 978-1-59473-263-8 **$16.99**

Hearing the Call across Traditions: Readings on Faith and Service
Edited by Adam Davis; Foreword by Eboo Patel
Explores the connections between faith, service and social justice through the prose, verse and sacred texts of the world's great faith traditions.
6 x 9, 352 pp, Quality PB, 978-1-59473-303-1 **$18.99**; HC, 978-1-59473-264-5 **$29.99**

How to Do Good & Avoid Evil: A Global Ethic from the Sources of Judaism
by Hans Küng and Rabbi Walter Homolka; Translated by Rev. Dr. John Bowden
6 x 9, 224 pp, HC, 978-1-59473-255-3 **$19.99**

Blessed Relief: What Christians Can Learn from Buddhists about Suffering
by Gordon Peerman 6 x 9, 208 pp, Quality PB, 978-1-59473-252-2 **$16.99**

The Changing Christian World: A Brief Introduction for Jews
by Rabbi Leonard A. Schoolman 5½ x 8½, 176 pp, Quality PB, 978-1-58023-344-6 **$16.99***

Christians & Jews in Dialogue: Learning in the Presence of the Other *by Mary C. Boys and Sara S. Lee; Foreword by Dorothy C. Bass* 6 x 9, 240 pp, Quality PB, 978-1-59473-254-6 **$18.99**

Disaster Spiritual Care: Practical Clergy Responses to Community, Regional and National Tragedy *Edited by Rabbi Stephen B. Roberts, BCJC, and Rev. Willard W.C. Ashley, Sr., DMin, DH* 6 x 9, 384 pp, HC, 978-1-59473-240-9 **$40.00**

InterActive Faith: The Essential Interreligious Community-Building Handbook
Edited by Rev. Bud Heckman with Rori Picker Neiss; Foreword by Rev. Dirk Ficca
6 x 9, 304 pp, Quality PB, 978-1-59473-273-7 **$16.99**; HC, 978-1-59473-237-9 **$29.99**

The Jewish Approach to God: A Brief Introduction for Christians
by Rabbi Neil Gillman, PhD 5½ x 8½, 192 pp, Quality PB, 978-1-58023-190-9 **$16.95***

The Jewish Approach to Repairing the World (*Tikkun Olam*): A Brief Introduction
for Christians *by Rabbi Elliot N. Dorff, PhD, with Rev. Cory Willson*
5½ x 8½, 256 pp, Quality PB, 978-1-58023-349-1 **$16.99***

The Jewish Connection to Israel, the Promised Land: A Brief Introduction for
Christians *by Rabbi Eugene Korn, PhD* 5½ x 8½, 192 pp, Quality PB, 978-1-58023-318-7 **$14.99***

Jewish Holidays: A Brief Introduction for Christians *by Rabbi Kerry M. Olitzky and Rabbi Daniel Judson* 5½ x 8½, 176 pp, Quality PB, 978-1-58023-302-6 **$16.99***

Jewish Ritual: A Brief Introduction for Christians
by Rabbi Kerry M. Olitzky and Rabbi Daniel Judson 5½ x 8½, 144 pp, Quality PB, 978-1-58023-210-4 **$14.99***

Jewish Spirituality: A Brief Introduction for Christians *by Rabbi Lawrence Kushner*
5½ x 8½, 112 pp, Quality PB, 978-1-58023-150-3 **$12.95***

A Jewish Understanding of the New Testament *by Rabbi Samuel Sandmel; New preface by Rabbi David Sandmel* 5½ x 8½, 368 pp, Quality PB, 978-1-59473-048-1 **$19.99***

Modern Jews Engage the New Testament: Enhancing Jewish Well-Being in a Christian Environment *by Rabbi Michael J. Cook, PhD* 6 x 9, 416 pp, HC, 978-1-58023-313-2 **$29.99***

Talking about God: Exploring the Meaning of Religious Life with Kierkegaard, Buber, Tillich and Heschel *by Daniel F. Polish, PhD* 6 x 9, 160 pp, Quality PB, 978-1-59473-272-0 **$16.99**

We Jews and Jesus: Exploring Theological Differences for Mutual Understanding
by Rabbi Samuel Sandmel; New preface by Rabbi David Sandmel
6 x 9, 192 pp, Quality PB, 978-1-59473-208-9 **$16.99**

Who Are the *Real* Chosen People? The Meaning of Chosenness in Judaism, Christianity and Islam *by Reuven Firestone, PhD*
6 x 9, 176 pp, Quality PB, 978-1-59473-290-4 **$16.99**; HC, 978-1-59473-248-5 **$21.99**

* A book from Jewish Lights, SkyLight Paths' sister imprint

Children's Spirituality

Adam & Eve's First Sunset: God's New Day
by Sandy Eisenberg Sasso; Full-color illus. by Joani Keller Rothenberg 9 x 12, 32 pp, Full-color illus., HC,
978-1-58023-177-0 **$17.95*** *For ages 4 & up*

Because Nothing Looks Like God
by Lawrence Kushner and Karen Kushner; Full-color illus. by Dawn W. Majewski
Invites parents and children to explore the questions we all have about God.
11 x 8½, 32 pp, Full-color illus., HC, 978-1-58023-092-6 **$17.99*** *For ages 4 & up*
Also available: **Teacher's Guide** 8½ x 11, 22 pp, PB, 978-1-58023-140-4 **$6.95**

But God Remembered: Stories of Women from Creation to the
Promised Land   *by Sandy Eisenberg Sasso; Full-color illus. by Bethanne Andersen*
A fascinating collection of four different stories of women only briefly
mentioned in biblical tradition and religious texts.
9 x 12, 32 pp, Full-color illus., Quality PB, 978-1-58023-372-9 **$8.99*** *For ages 8 & up*

Cain & Abel: Finding the Fruits of Peace
by Sandy Eisenberg Sasso; Full-color illus. by Joani Keller Rothenberg
A sensitive recasting of the ancient tale shows we have the power to deal with anger
in positive ways. "Editor's Choice." —American Library Association's *Booklist*
9 x 12, 32 pp, Full-color illus., HC, 978-1-58023-123-7 **$16.95*** *For ages 5 & up*

Does God Hear My Prayer?
by August Gold; Full-color photos by Diane Hardy Waller
Introduces preschoolers and young readers to prayer and how it helps them
express their own emotions.
10 x 8½, 32 pp, Full-color photo illus., Quality PB, 978-1-59473-102-0 **$8.99** *For ages 3–6*

The 11th Commandment: Wisdom from Our Children *by The Children of America*
"If there were an Eleventh Commandment, what would it be?" Children of many
religious denominations across America answer this question—in their own draw-
ings and words. "A rare book of spiritual celebration for all people, of all ages,
for all time." —*Bookviews* 8 x 10, 48 pp, Full-color illus., HC, 978-1-879045-46-0 **$16.95***
For all ages

For Heaven's Sake *by Sandy Eisenberg Sasso; Full-color illus. by Kathryn Kunz Finney*
Heaven is often found where you least expect it.
9 x 12, 32 pp, Full-color illus., HC, 978-1-58023-054-4 **$16.95*** *For ages 4 & up*

God in Between *by Sandy Eisenberg Sasso; Full-color illus. by Sally Sweetland*
A magical, mythical tale that teaches that God can be found where we are.
9 x 12, 32 pp, Full-color illus., HC, 978-1-879045-86-6 **$16.95*** *For ages 4 & up*

God's Paintbrush: Special 10th Anniversary Edition
by Sandy Eisenberg Sasso; Full-color illus. by Annette Compton
Invites children of all faiths and backgrounds to encounter God through moments in
their own lives. 11 x 8½, 32 pp, Full-color illus., HC, 978-1-58023-195-4 **$17.95*** *For ages 4 & up*

Also available: **God's Paintbrush Teacher's Guide**
8½ x 11, 32 pp, PB, 978-1-879045-57-6 **$8.95**

God's Paintbrush Celebration Kit: A Spiritual Activity Kit for Teachers and
Students of All Faiths, All Backgrounds 9½ x 12, 40 Full-color Activity Sheets & Teacher Folder
w/ complete instructions, HC, 978-1-58023-050-6 **$21.95**
Additional activity sheets available:
8-Student Activity Sheet Pack (40 sheets/5 sessions), 978-1-58023-058-2 **$19.95**
Single-Student Activity Sheet Pack (5 sessions), 978-1-58023-059-9 **$3.95**

I Am God's Paintbrush (A Board Book)
by Sandy Eisenberg Sasso; Full-color illus. by Annette Compton
5 x 5, 24 pp, Full-color illus., Board Book, 978-1-59473-265-2 **$7.99** *For ages 0–4*

* A book from Jewish Lights, SkyLight Paths' sister imprint

Children's Spirituality

Remembering My Grandparent: A Kid's Own Grief Workbook in the Christian Tradition *by Nechama Liss-Levinson, PhD, and Rev. Molly Phinney Baskette, MDiv* 8 x 10, 48 pp, 2-color text, HC, 978-1-59473-212-6 **$16.99** *For ages 7 & up*

Does God Ever Sleep? *by Joan Sauro, CSJ*
A charming nighttime reminder that God is always present in our lives.
10 x 8½, 32 pp, Full-color photos, Quality PB, 978-1-59473-110-5 **$8.99** *For ages 3–6*

Does God Forgive Me? *by August Gold; Full-color photos by Diane Hardy Waller*
Gently shows how God forgives all that we do if we are truly sorry.
10 x 8½, 32 pp, Full-color photos, Quality PB, 978-1-59473-142-6 **$8.99** *For ages 3–6*

God Said Amen *by Sandy Eisenberg Sasso; Full-color illus. by Avi Katz*
A warm and inspiring tale that shows us that we need only reach out to each other to find the answers to our prayers.
9 x 12, 32 pp, Full-color illus., HC, 978-1-58023-080-3 **$16.95*** *For ages 4 & up*

How Does God Listen? *by Kay Lindahl; Full-color photos by Cynthia Maloney*
How do we know when God is listening to us? Children will find the answers to these questions as they engage their senses while the story unfolds, learning how God listens in the wind, waves, clouds, hot chocolate, perfume, our tears and our laughter.
10 x 8½, 32 pp, Full-color photos, Quality PB, 978-1-59473-084-9 **$8.99** *For ages 3–6*

In God's Hands *by Lawrence Kushner and Gary Schmidt; Full-color illus. by Matthew J. Baek*
9 x 12, 32 pp, Full-color illus., HC, 978-1-58023-224-1 **$16.99*** *For ages 5 & up*

In God's Name *by Sandy Eisenberg Sasso; Full-color illus. by Phoebe Stone*
Like an ancient myth in its poetic text and vibrant illustrations, this award-winning modern fable about the search for God's name celebrates the diversity and, at the same time, the unity of all the people of the world.
9 x 12, 32 pp, Full-color illus., HC, 978-1-879045-26-2 **$16.99*** *For ages 4 & up*

Also available in Spanish: **El nombre de Dios**
9 x 12, 32 pp, Full-color illus., HC, 978-1-893361-63-8 **$16.95**

In Our Image: God's First Creatures
by Nancy Sohn Swartz; Full-color illus. by Melanie Hall
A playful new twist on the Genesis story—from the perspective of the animals. Celebrates the interconnectedness of nature and the harmony of all living things.
9 x 12, 32 pp, Full-color illus., HC, 978-1-879045-99-6 **$16.95*** *For ages 4 & up*

Noah's Wife: The Story of Naamah
by Sandy Eisenberg Sasso; Full-color illus. by Bethanne Andersen
Opens young readers' religious imaginations to new ideas about the well-known story of the Flood. When God tells Noah to bring the animals of the world onto the ark, God also calls on Naamah, Noah's wife, to save each plant on Earth.
9 x 12, 32 pp, Full-color illus., HC, 978-1-58023-134-3 **$16.95*** *For ages 4 & up*

Also available: **Naamah:** Noah's Wife (A Board Book)
by Sandy Eisenberg Sasso; Full-color illus. by Bethanne Andersen
5 x 5, 24 pp, Full-color illus., Board Book, 978-1-893361-56-0 **$7.95** *For ages 0–4*

Where Does God Live? *by August Gold and Matthew J. Perlman*
Helps children and their parents find God in the world around us with simple, practical examples children can relate to.
10 x 8½, 32 pp, Full-color photos, Quality PB, 978-1-893361-39-3 **$8.99** *For ages 3–6*

* A book from Jewish Lights, SkyLight Paths' sister imprint

Children's Spirituality—Board Books

Adam & Eve's New Day
by Sandy Eisenberg Sasso; Full-color illus. by Joani Keller Rothenberg
A lesson in hope for every child who has worried about what comes next.
Abridged from *Adam & Eve's First Sunset.*
5 x 5, 24 pp, Full-color illus., Board Book, 978-1-59473-205-8 **$7.99** *For ages 0–4*

How Did the Animals Help God?
by Nancy Sohn Swartz; Full-color illus. by Melanie Hall
God asks all of nature to offer gifts to humankind—with a promise that they will
care for creation in return. Abridged from *In Our Image.*
5 x 5, 24 pp, Full-color illus., Board Book, 978-1-59473-044-3 **$7.99** *For ages 0–4*

How Does God Make Things Happen?
by Lawrence and Karen Kushner; Full-color illus. by Dawn W. Majewski
A charming invitation for young children to explore how God makes things happen in
our world. Abridged from *Because Nothing Looks Like God.*
5 x 5, 24 pp, Full-color illus., Board Book, 978-1-893361-24-9 **$7.95** *For ages 0–4*

What Does God Look Like?
by Lawrence and Karen Kushner; Full-color illus. by Dawn W. Majewski
A simple way for young children to explore the ways that we "see" God. Abridged
from *Because Nothing Looks Like God.*
5 x 5, 24 pp, Full-color illus., Board Book, 978-1-893361-23-2 **$7.99** *For ages 0–4*

What Is God's Name?
by Sandy Eisenberg Sasso; Full-color illus. by Phoebe Stone
Everyone and everything in the world has a name. What is God's name? Abridged
from the award-winning *In God's Name.*
5 x 5, 24 pp, Full-color illus., Board Book, 978-1-893361-10-2 **$7.99** *For ages 0–4*

Where Is God? *by Lawrence and Karen Kushner; Full-color illus. by*
Dawn W. Majewski A gentle way for young children to explore how God is with
us every day, in every way. Abridged from *Because Nothing Looks Like God.*
5 x 5, 24 pp, Full-color illus., Board Book, 978-1-893361-17-1 **$7.99** *For ages 0–4*

What You Will See Inside ...

Fun-to-read books with vibrant full-color photos show children ages 6
and up the who, what, when, where, why and how of traditional
houses of worship, liturgical celebrations and rituals of different world
faiths, empowering them to respect and understand their own religious
traditions—and those of their friends and neighbors.

What You Will See Inside a Catholic Church
by Rev. Michael Keane; Foreword by Robert J. Kealey, EdD
Full-color photos by Aaron Pepis
8½ x 10½, 32 pp, Full-color photos, HC, 978-1-893361-54-6 **$17.95**

Also available in Spanish: **Lo que se puede ver dentro de una iglesia católica**
8½ x 10½, 32 pp, Full-color photos, HC, 978-1-893361-66-9 **$16.95**

What You Will See Inside a Hindu Temple
by Mahendra Jani, PhD, and Vandana Jani, PhD; Full-color photos by Neirah Bhargava and Vijay Dave
8½ x 10½, 32 pp, Full-color photos, HC, 978-1-59473-116-7 **$17.99**

What You Will See Inside a Mosque
by Aisha Karen Khan; Full-color photos by Aaron Pepis
8½ x 10½, 32 pp, Full-color photos, Quality PB, 978-1-59473-257-7 **$8.99**

What You Will See Inside a Synagogue
by Rabbi Lawrence A. Hoffman, PhD, and Dr. Ron Wolfson; Full-color photos by Bill Aron
8½ x 10½, 32 pp, Full-color photos, Quality PB, 978-1-59473-256-0 **$8.99**

Children's Spiritual Biography

Ten Amazing People
And How They Changed the World
by Maura D. Shaw; Foreword by Dr. Robert Coles
Full-color illus. by Stephen Marchesi

For ages 7 & up

Shows kids that spiritual people can have an exciting impact on the world around them. Kids will delight in reading about these amazing people and what they accomplished through their words and actions.

Black Elk • Dorothy Day • Malcolm X • Mahatma Gandhi • Martin Luther King, Jr. • Mother Teresa • Janusz Korczak • Desmond Tutu • Thich Nhat Hanh • Albert Schweitzer

"Best Juvenile/Young Adult Non-Fiction Book of the Year."
—*Independent Publisher*

"Will inspire adults and children alike."
—*Globe and Mail* (Toronto)

8½ x 11, 48 pp, Full-color illus., HC, 978-1-893361-47-8 **$17.95** *For ages 7 & up*

Spiritual Biographies for Young People
For Ages 7 & Up

By Maura D. Shaw; Illus. by Stephen Marchesi
6¼ x 8¾, 32 pp, Full-color and b/w illus., HC

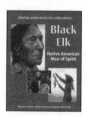
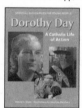
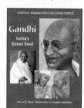
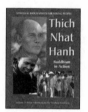

Black Elk: Native American Man of Spirit
Through historically accurate illustrations and photos, inspiring age-appropriate activities and Black Elk's own words, this colorful biography introduces children to a remarkable person who ensured that the traditions and beliefs of his people would not be forgotten.
978-1-59473-043-6 **$12.99**

Dorothy Day: A Catholic Life of Action
Introduces children to one of the most inspiring women of the twentieth century, a down-to-earth spiritual leader who saw the presence of God in every person she met. Includes practical activities, a timeline and a list of important words to know.
978-1-59473-011-5 **$12.99**

Gandhi: India's Great Soul
The only biography of Gandhi that balances a simple text with illustrations, photos and activities that encourage children and adults to talk about how to make changes happen without violence. Introduces children to important concepts of freedom, equality and justice among people of all backgrounds and religions.
978-1-893361-91-1 **$12.95**

Thich Nhat Hanh: Buddhism in Action
Warm illustrations, photos, age-appropriate activities and Thich Nhat Hanh's own poems introduce a great man to children in a way they can understand and enjoy. Includes a list of important Buddhist words to know.
978-1-893361-87-4 **$12.95**

Bible Stories / Folktales

Abraham's Bind & Other Bible Tales of Trickery, Folly, Mercy and Love by Michael J. Caduto
New retellings of episodes in the lives of familiar biblical characters explore relevant life lessons.   6 x 9, 224 pp, HC, 978-1-59473-186-0 **$19.99**

Daughters of the Desert: Stories of Remarkable Women from Christian, Jewish and Muslim Traditions by Claire Rudolf Murphy,
Meghan Nuttall Sayres, Mary Cronk Farrell, Sarah Conover and Betsy Wharton
Breathes new life into the old tales of our female ancestors in faith. Uses traditional scriptural passages as starting points, then with vivid detail fills in historical context and place. Chapters reveal the voices of Sarah, Hagar, Huldah, Esther, Salome, Mary Magdalene, Lydia, Khadija, Fatima and many more. Historical fiction ideal for readers of all ages.
5½ x 8½, 192 pp, Quality PB, 978-1-59473-106-8 **$14.99**   Inc. reader's discussion guide
HC, 978-1-893361-72-0 **$19.95**

The Triumph of Eve & Other Subversive Bible Tales
by Matt Biers-Ariel
These engaging retellings of familiar Bible stories are witty, often hilarious and always profound. They invite you to grapple with questions and issues that are often hidden in the original texts.
5½ x 8½, 192 pp, Quality PB, 978-1-59473-176-1 **$14.99**
Also available: **The Triumph of Eve Teacher's Guide**
8½ x 11, 44 pp, PB, 978-1-59473-152-5 **$8.99**

Wisdom in the Telling
Finding Inspiration and Grace in Traditional Folktales and Myths Retold
by Lorraine Hartin-Gelardi
6 x 9, 192 pp, HC, 978-1-59473-185-3 **$19.99**

Religious Etiquette / Reference

How to Be a Perfect Stranger, 5th Edition: The Essential Religious Etiquette Handbook Edited by Stuart M. Matlins and Arthur J. Magida
The indispensable guidebook to help the well-meaning guest when visiting other people's religious ceremonies. A straightforward guide to the rituals and celebrations of the major religions and denominations in the United States and Canada from the perspective of an interested guest of any other faith, based on information obtained from authorities of each religion. Belongs in every living room, library and office. Covers: **African American Methodist Churches • Assemblies of God • Bahá'í Faith • Baptist • Buddhist • Christian Church (Disciples of Christ) • Christian Science (Church of Christ, Scientist) • Churches of Christ • Episcopalian and Anglican • Hindu • Islam • Jehovah's Witnesses • Jewish • Lutheran • Mennonite/Amish • Methodist • Mormon (Church of Jesus Christ of Latter-day Saints) • Native American/First Nations • Orthodox Churches • Pentecostal Church of God • Presbyterian • Quaker (Religious Society of Friends) • Reformed Church in America/Canada • Roman Catholic • Seventh-day Adventist • Sikh • Unitarian Universalist • United Church of Canada • United Church of Christ**

"The things Miss Manners forgot to tell us about religion."

—*Los Angeles Times*

"Finally, for those inclined to undertake their own spiritual journeys ... tells visitors what to expect.   —*New York Times*

6 x 9, 432 pp, Quality PB, 978-1-59473-294-2 **$19.99**

The Perfect Stranger's Guide to Funerals and Grieving Practices: A Guide to Etiquette in Other People's Religious Ceremonies Edited by Stuart M. Matlins
6 x 9, 240 pp, Quality PB, 978-1-893361-20-1 **$16.95**

The Perfect Stranger's Guide to Wedding Ceremonies: A Guide to Etiquette in Other People's Religious Ceremonies Edited by Stuart M. Matlins
6 x 9, 208 pp, Quality PB, 978-1-893361-19-5 **$16.95**

Sacred Texts—SkyLight Illuminations Series

Offers today's spiritual seeker an enjoyable entry into the great classic texts of the world's spiritual traditions. Each classic is presented in an accessible translation, with facing pages of guided commentary from experts, giving you the keys you need to understand the history, context and meaning of the text.

CHRISTIANITY

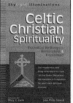

Celtic Christian Spirituality: Essential Writings—Annotated & Explained
Annotation by Mary C. Earle; Foreword by John Philip Newell
Explores how the writings of this lively tradition embody the gospel.
5½ x 8½, 160 pp, Quality PB, 978-1-59473-302-4 **$16.99**

The End of Days: Essential Selections from Apocalyptic Texts—
Annotated & Explained *Annotation by Robert G. Clouse, PhD*
Helps you understand the complex Christian visions of the end of the world.
5½ x 8½, 224 pp, Quality PB, 978-1-59473-170-9 **$16.99**

The Hidden Gospel of Matthew: Annotated & Explained
Translation & Annotation by Ron Miller Discover the words and events that have the strongest connection to the historical Jesus.
5½ x 8½, 272 pp, Quality PB, 978-1-59473-038-2 **$16.99**

The Infancy Gospels of Jesus: Apocryphal Tales from the Childhoods of Mary and Jesus—Annotated & Explained
Translation & Annotation by Stevan Davies; Foreword by A. Edward Siecienski, PhD
A startling presentation of the early lives of Mary, Jesus and other biblical figures that will amuse and surprise you. 5½ x 8½, 176 pp, Quality PB, 978-1-59473-258-4 **$16.99**

The Lost Sayings of Jesus: Teachings from Ancient Christian, Jewish, Gnostic and Islamic Sources—Annotated & Explained
Translation & Annotation by Andrew Phillip Smith; Foreword by Stephan A. Hoeller
This collection of more than three hundred sayings depicts Jesus as a Wisdom teacher who speaks to people of all faiths as a mystic and spiritual master.
5½ x 8½, 240 pp, Quality PB, 978-1-59473-172-3 **$16.99**

Philokalia: The Eastern Christian Spiritual Texts—Selections Annotated & Explained *Annotation by Allyne Smith; Translation by G. E. H. Palmer, Phillip Sherrard and Bishop Kallistos Ware*
The first approachable introduction to the wisdom of the Philokalia, the classic text of Eastern Christian spirituality. 5½ x 8½, 240 pp, Quality PB, 978-1-59473-103-7 **$16.99**

The Sacred Writings of Paul: Selections Annotated & Explained
Translation & Annotation by Ron Miller Leads you into the exciting immediacy of Paul's teachings. 5½ x 8½, 224 pp, Quality PB, 978-1-59473-213-3 **$16.99**

Saint Augustine of Hippo: Selections from *Confessions* and Other Essential Writings—Annotated & Explained
Annotation by Joseph T. Kelley, PhD; Translation by the Augustinian Heritage Institute
Provides insight into the mind and heart of this foundational Christian figure.
5½ x 8½, 272 pp, Quality PB, 978-1-59473-282-9 **$16.99**

St. Ignatius Loyola—The Spiritual Writings: Selections Annotated & Explained *Annotation by Mark Mossa, SJ*
Draws from contemporary translations of original texts focusing on the practical mysticism of Ignatius of Loyola. 5½ x 8½, 224 pp (est), Quality PB, 978-1-59473-301-7 **$16.99**

Sex Texts from the Bible: Selections Annotated & Explained
Translation & Annotation by Teresa J. Hornsby; Foreword by Amy-Jill Levine
Demystifies the Bible's ideas on gender roles, marriage, sexual orientation, virginity, lust and sexual pleasure. 5½ x 8½, 208 pp, Quality PB, 978-1-59473-217-1 **$16.99**

Sacred Texts—continued

CHRISTIANITY—continued

Spiritual Writings on Mary: Annotated & Explained
Annotation by Mary Ford-Grabowsky; Foreword by Andrew Harvey
Examines the role of Mary, the mother of Jesus, as a source of inspiration in history and in life today. 5½ x 8½, 288 pp, Quality PB, 978-1-59473-001-6 **$16.99**

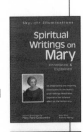

The Way of a Pilgrim: The Jesus Prayer Journey—Annotated & Explained
Translation & Annotation by Gleb Pokrovsky; Foreword by Andrew Harvey
A classic of Russian Orthodox spirituality.
5½ x 8½, 160 pp, Illus., Quality PB, 978-1-893361-31-7 **$14.95**

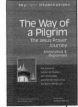

GNOSTICISM

Gnostic Writings on the Soul: Annotated & Explained
Translation & Annotation by Andrew Phillip Smith; Foreword by Stephan A. Hoeller
Reveals the inspiring ways your soul can remember and return to its unique, divine purpose. 5½ x 8½, 144 pp, Quality PB, 978-1-59473-220-1 **$16.99**

The Gospel of Philip: Annotated & Explained
Translation & Annotation by Andrew Phillip Smith; Foreword by Stevan Davies
Reveals otherwise unrecorded sayings of Jesus and fragments of Gnostic mythology.
5½ x 8½, 160 pp, Quality PB, 978-1-59473-111-2 **$16.99**

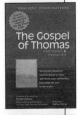

The Gospel of Thomas: Annotated & Explained
Translation & Annotation by Stevan Davies; Foreword by Andrew Harvey
Sheds new light on the origins of Christianity and portrays Jesus as a wisdom-loving sage.
5½ x 8½, 192 pp, Quality PB, 978-1-893361-45-4 **$16.99**

The Secret Book of John: The Gnostic Gospel—Annotated & Explained
Translation & Annotation by Stevan Davies The most significant and influential text of the ancient Gnostic religion. 5½ x 8½, 208 pp, Quality PB, 978-1-59473-082-5 **$16.99**

JUDAISM

The Divine Feminine in Biblical Wisdom Literature
Selections Annotated & Explained
Translation & Annotation by Rabbi Rami Shapiro; Foreword by Rev. Cynthia Bourgeault, PhD
Uses the Hebrew Bible and Wisdom literature to explain Sophia's way of wisdom and illustrate Her creative energy. 5½ x 8½, 240 pp, Quality PB, 978-1-59473-109-9 **$16.99**

Ecclesiastes: Annotated & Explained
Translation & Annotation by Rabbi Rami Shapiro; Foreword by Rev. Barbara Cawthorne Crafton
A timeless teaching on living well amid uncertainty and insecurity.
5½ x 8½, 160 pp, Quality PB, 978-1-59473-287-4 **$16.99**

Ethics of the Sages: *Pirke Avot*—Annotated & Explained
Translation & Annotation by Rabbi Rami Shapiro Clarifies the ethical teachings of the early Rabbis. 5½ x 8½, 192 pp, Quality PB, 978-1-59473-207-2 **$16.99**

Hasidic Tales: Annotated & Explained
Translation & Annotation by Rabbi Rami Shapiro; Foreword by Andrew Harvey
Introduces the legendary tales of the impassioned Hasidic rabbis, presenting them as stories rather than as parables. 5½ x 8½, 240 pp, Quality PB, 978-1-893361-86-7 **$16.95**

The Hebrew Prophets: Selections Annotated & Explained
Translation & Annotation by Rabbi Rami Shapiro; Foreword by Rabbi Zalman M. Schachter-Shalomi
5½ x 8½, 224 pp, Quality PB, 978-1-59473-037-5 **$16.99**

Tanya, the Masterpiece of Hasidic Wisdom: Selections Annotated & Explained *Translation & Annotation by Rabbi Rami Shapiro; Foreword by Rabbi Zalman M. Schachter-Shalomi* Clarifies one of the most powerful and potentially transformative books of Jewish wisdom. 5½ x 8½, 240 pp, Quality PB, 978-1-59473-275-1 **$16.99**

Zohar: Annotated & Explained *Translation & Annotation by Daniel C. Matt; Foreword by Andrew Harvey* The canonical text of Jewish mystical tradition.
5½ x 8½, 176 pp, Quality PB, 978-1-893361-51-5 **$15.99**

Sacred Texts—continued

ISLAM

Ghazali on the Principles of Islamic Spirituality
Selections from *Forty Foundations of Religion*—Annotated & Explained
Translation & Annotation by Aaron Spevack, PhD
Makes the core message of this influential spiritual master relevant to anyone seeking a balanced understanding of Islam.
5½ x 8½, 208 pp (est), Quality PB, 978-1-59473-284-3 **$16.99**

The Qur'an and Sayings of Prophet Muhammad
Selections Annotated & Explained
Annotation by Sohaib N. Sultan; Translation by Yusuf Ali, Revised by Sohaib N. Sultan; Foreword by Jane I. Smith
Presents the foundational wisdom of Islam in an easy-to-use format.
5½ x 8½, 256 pp, Quality PB, 978-1-59473-222-5 **$16.99**

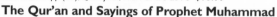

Rumi and Islam: Selections from His Stories, Poems, and Discourses—
Annotated & Explained *Translation & Annotation by Ibrahim Gamard*
Focuses on Rumi's place within the Sufi tradition of Islam, providing insight into the mystical side of the religion.
5½ x 8½, 240 pp, Quality PB, 978-1-59473-002-3 **$15.99**

EASTERN RELIGIONS

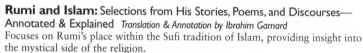

The Art of War—Spirituality for Conflict: Annotated & Explained
by Sun Tzu; Annotation by Thomas Huynh; Translation by Thomas Huynh and the Editors at Sonshi.com; Foreword by Marc Benioff; Preface by Thomas Cleary
Highlights principles that encourage a perceptive and spiritual approach to conflict.
5½ x 8½, 256 pp, Quality PB, 978-1-59473-244-7 **$16.99**

Bhagavad Gita: Annotated & Explained
Translation by Shri Purohit Swami; Annotation by Kendra Crossen Burroughs; Foreword by Andrew Harvey
Presents the classic text's teachings—with no previous knowledge of Hinduism required.
5½ x 8½, 192 pp, Quality PB, 978-1-893361-28-7 **$16.95**

Chuang-tzu: The Tao of Perfect Happiness—Selections Annotated & Explained
Translation & Annotation by Livia Kohn, PhD
Presents Taoism's central message of reverence for the "Way" of the natural world.
5½ x 8½, 240 pp, Quality PB, 978-1-59473-296-6 **$16.99**

Confucius, the *Analects:* The Path of the Sage—Selections Annotated & Explained
Annotation by Rodney L Taylor, PhD; Translation by James Legge, Revised by Rodney L Taylor, PhD Explores the ethical and spiritual meaning behind the Confucian way of learning and self-cultivation.
5½ x 8½, 192 pp, Quality PB, 978-1-59473-306-2 **$16.99**

Dhammapada: Annotated & Explained
Translation by Max Müller, revised by Jack Maguire; Annotation by Jack Maguire; Foreword by Andrew Harvey Contains all of Buddhism's key teachings, plus commentary that explains all the names, terms and references.
5½ x 8½, 160 pp, b/w photos, Quality PB, 978-1-893361-42-3 **$14.95**

Selections from the Gospel of Sri Ramakrishna: Annotated & Explained
Translation by Swami Nikhilananda; Annotation by Kendra Crossen Burroughs; Foreword by Andrew Harvey Introduces the fascinating world of the Indian mystic and the universal appeal of his message.
5½ x 8½, 240 pp, b/w photos, Quality PB, 978-1-893361-46-1 **$16.95**

Tao Te Ching: Annotated & Explained
Translation & Annotation by Derek Lin; Foreword by Lama Surya Das
Introduces an Eastern classic in an accessible, poetic and completely original way.
5½ x 8½, 208 pp, Quality PB, 978-1-59473-204-1 **$16.99**

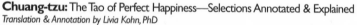

Spirituality of the Seasons

Autumn: A Spiritual Biography of the Season
Edited by Gary Schmidt and Susan M. Felch; Illus. by Mary Azarian
Rejoice in autumn as a time of preparation and reflection. Includes Wendell Berry, David James Duncan, Robert Frost, A. Bartlett Giamatti, E. B. White, P. D. James, Julian of Norwich, Garret Keizer, Tracy Kidder, Anne Lamott, May Sarton.
6 x 9, 320 pp, b/w illus., Quality PB, 978-1-59473-118-1 **$18.99**

Spring: A Spiritual Biography of the Season
Edited by Gary Schmidt and Susan M. Felch; Illus. by Mary Azarian
Explore the gentle unfurling of spring and reflect on how nature celebrates rebirth and renewal. Includes Jane Kenyon, Lucy Larcom, Harry Thurston, Nathaniel Hawthorne, Noel Perrin, Annie Dillard, Martha Ballard, Barbara Kingsolver, Dorothy Wordsworth, Donald Hall, David Brill, Lionel Basney, Isak Dinesen, Paul Laurence Dunbar. 6 x 9, 352 pp, b/w illus., Quality PB, 978-1-59473-246-1 **$18.99**

Summer: A Spiritual Biography of the Season
Edited by Gary Schmidt and Susan M. Felch; Illus. by Barry Moser
"A sumptuous banquet.... These selections lift up an exquisite wholeness found within an everyday sophistication." — ★ *Publishers Weekly* starred review
Includes Anne Lamott, Luci Shaw, Ray Bradbury, Richard Selzer, Thomas Lynch, Walt Whitman, Carl Sandburg, Sherman Alexie, Madeleine L'Engle, Jamaica Kincaid.
6 x 9, 304 pp, b/w illus., Quality PB, 978-1-59473-183-9 **$18.99**
HC, 978-1-59473-083-2 **$21.99**

Winter: A Spiritual Biography of the Season
Edited by Gary Schmidt and Susan M. Felch; Illus. by Barry Moser
"This outstanding anthology features top-flight nature and spirituality writers on the fierce, inexorable season of winter.... Remarkably lively and warm, despite the icy subject." — ★ *Publishers Weekly* starred review
Includes Will Campbell, Rachel Carson, Annie Dillard, Donald Hall, Ron Hansen, Jane Kenyon, Jamaica Kincaid, Barry Lopez, Kathleen Norris, John Updike, E. B. White.
6 x 9, 288 pp, b/w illus., Deluxe PB w/ flaps, 978-1-893361-92-8 **$18.95**
HC, 978-1-893361-53-9 **$21.95**

Spirituality / Animal Companions

Blessing the Animals: Prayers and Ceremonies to Celebrate God's Creatures, Wild and Tame *Edited and with Introductions by Lynn L. Caruso*
5¼ x 7¼, 256 pp, Quality PB, 978-1-59473-253-9 **$15.99**; HC, 978-1-59473-145-7 **$19.99**

Remembering My Pet: A Kid's Own Spiritual Workbook for When a Pet Dies
by Nechama Liss-Levinson, PhD, and Rev. Molly Phinney Baskette, MDiv; Foreword by Lynn L. Caruso
8 x 10, 48 pp, 2-color text, HC, 978-1-59473-221-8 **$16.99**

What Animals Can Teach Us about Spirituality: Inspiring Lessons from Wild and Tame Creatures *by Diana L. Guerrero* 6 x 9, 176 pp, Quality PB, 978-1-893361-84-3 **$16.95**

Spirituality—A Week Inside

Lighting the Lamp of Wisdom: A Week Inside a Yoga Ashram
by John Ittner; Foreword by Dr. David Frawley
6 x 9, 192 pp, b/w photos, Quality PB, 978-1-893361-52-2 **$15.95**

Making a Heart for God: A Week Inside a Catholic Monastery
by Dianne Aprile; Foreword by Brother Patrick Hart, OCSO
6 x 9, 224 pp, b/w photos, Quality PB, 978-1-893361-49-2 **$16.95**

Waking Up: A Week Inside a Zen Monastery
by Jack Maguire; Foreword by John Daido Loori, Roshi
6 x 9, 224 pp, b/w photos, Quality PB, 978-1-893361-55-3 **$16.95**; HC, 978-1-893361-13-3 **$21.95**

Spirituality

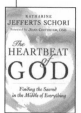

The Heartbeat of God: Finding the Sacred in the Middle of Everything
by Katharine Jefferts Schori; Foreword by Joan Chittister, OSB
Explores our connections to other people, to other nations and with the environment through the lens of faith. 6 x 9, 240 pp, HC, 978-1-59473-292-8 **$21.99**

A Dangerous Dozen: Twelve Christians Who Threatened the Status Quo but Taught Us to Live Like Jesus
by the Rev. Canon C. K. Robertson, PhD; Foreword by Archbishop Desmond Tutu
Profiles twelve visionary men and women who challenged society and showed the world a different way of living. 6 x 9, 208 pp, Quality PB, 978-1-59473-298-0 **$16.99**

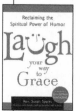

Decision Making & Spiritual Discernment: The Sacred Art of Finding Your Way *by Nancy L. Bieber*
Presents three essential aspects of Spirit-led decision making: willingness, attentiveness and responsiveness. 5½ x 8½, 208 pp, Quality PB, 978-1-59473-289-8 **$16.99**

Laugh Your Way to Grace: Reclaiming the Spiritual Power of Humor
by Rev. Susan Sparks A powerful, humorous case for laughter as a spiritual, healing path. 6 x 9, 176 pp, Quality PB, 978-1-59473-280-5 **$16.99**

Living into Hope: A Call to Spiritual Action for Such a Time as This
by Rev. Dr. Joan Brown Campbell; Foreword by Karen Armstrong
A visionary minister speaks out on the pressing issues that face us today, offering inspiration and challenge. 6 x 9, 208 pp, HC, 978-1-59473-283-6 **$21.99**

Claiming Earth as Common Ground: The Ecological Crisis through the Lens of Faith
by Andrea Cohen-Kiener; Foreword by Rev. Sally Bingham
6 x 9, 192 pp, Quality PB, 978-1-59473-261-4 **$16.99**

Bread, Body, Spirit: Finding the Sacred in Food
Edited and with Introductions by Alice Peck 6 x 9, 224 pp, Quality PB, 978-1-59473-242-3 **$19.99**

Creating a Spiritual Retirement: A Guide to the Unseen Possibilities in Our Lives
by Molly Srode 6 x 9, 208 pp, b/w photos, Quality PB, 978-1-59473-050-4 **$14.99**

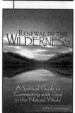

Creative Aging: Rethinking Retirement and Non-Retirement in a Changing World
by Marjory Zoet Bankson 6 x 9, 160 pp, Quality PB, 978-1-59473-281-2 **$16.99**

Keeping Spiritual Balance as We Grow Older: More than 65 Creative Ways to Use Purpose, Prayer, and the Power of Spirit to Build a Meaningful Retirement
by Molly and Bernie Srode 8 x 8, 224 pp, Quality PB, 978-1-59473-042-9 **$16.99**

Hearing the Call across Traditions: Readings on Faith and Service
Edited by Adam Davis; Foreword by Eboo Patel
6 x 9, 352 pp, Quality PB, 978-1-59473-303-1 **$18.99**; HC, 978-1-59473-264-5 **$29.99**

Honoring Motherhood: Prayers, Ceremonies & Blessings
Edited and with Introductions by Lynn L. Caruso 5 x 7¼, 272 pp, HC, 978-1-59473-239-3 **$19.99**

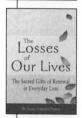

Journeys of Simplicity: Traveling Light with Thomas Merton, Bashō, Edward Abbey, Annie Dillard & Others *by Philip Harnden*
5 x 7¼, 144 pp, Quality PB, 978-1-59473-181-5 **$12.99**; 128 pp, HC, 978-1-893361-76-8 **$16.95**

The Losses of Our Lives: The Sacred Gifts of Renewal in Everyday Loss
by Dr. Nancy Copeland-Payton 6 x 9, 192 pp, HC, 978-1-59473-271-3 **$19.99**

Renewal in the Wilderness: A Spiritual Guide to Connecting with God in the Natural World *by John Lionberger*
6 x 9, 176 pp, b/w photos, Quality PB, 978-1-59473-219-5 **$16.99**

Soul Fire: Accessing Your Creativity
by Thomas Ryan, CSP 6 x 9, 160 pp, Quality PB, 978-1-59473-243-0 **$16.99**

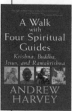

A Spirituality for Brokenness: Discovering Your Deepest Self in Difficult Times
by Terry Taylor 6 x 9, 176 pp, Quality PB, 978-1-59473-229-4 **$16.99**

A Walk with Four Spiritual Guides: Krishna, Buddha, Jesus, and Ramakrishna
by Andrew Harvey 5½ x 8½, 192 pp, b/w photos & illus., Quality PB, 978-1-59473-138-9 **$15.99**

The Workplace and Spirituality: New Perspectives on Research and Practice
Edited by Dr. Joan Marques, Dr. Satinder Dhiman and Dr. Richard King
6 x 9, 256 pp, HC, 978-1-59473-260-7 **$29.99**

Spirituality & Crafts

Beading—The Creative Spirit: Finding Your Sacred Center through the Art of Beadwork *by Rev. Wendy Ellsworth*
Invites you on a spiritual pilgrimage into the kaleidoscope world of glass and color.   7 × 9, 240 pp, 8-page color insert, 40+ b/w photos and 40 diagrams, Quality PB, 978-1-59473-267-6 **$18.99**

Contemplative Crochet: A Hands-On Guide for Interlocking Faith and Craft *by Cindy Crandall-Frazier; Foreword by Linda Skolnik*
Illuminates the spiritual lessons you can learn through crocheting.
7 × 9, 208 pp, b/w photos, Quality PB, 978-1-59473-238-6 **$16.99**

The Knitting Way: A Guide to Spiritual Self-Discovery
by Linda Skolnik and Janice MacDaniels Examines how you can explore and strengthen your spiritual life through knitting.
7 × 9, 240 pp, b/w photos, Quality PB, 978-1-59473-079-5 **$16.99**

The Painting Path: Embodying Spiritual Discovery through Yoga, Brush and Color *by Linda Novick; Foreword by Richard Segalman*
Explores the divine connection you can experience through art.
7 × 9, 208 pp, 8-page color insert, plus b/w photos,
Quality PB, 978-1-59473-226-3 **$18.99**

The Quilting Path: A Guide to Spiritual Discovery through Fabric, Thread and Kabbalah *by Louise Silk*
Explores how to cultivate personal growth through quilt making.
7 × 9, 192 pp, b/w photos and illus., Quality PB, 978-1-59473-206-5 **$16.99**

The Scrapbooking Journey: A Hands-On Guide to Spiritual Discovery
by Cory Richardson-Lauve; Foreword by Stacy Julian   Reveals how this craft can become a practice used to deepen and shape your life.
7 × 9, 176 pp, 8-page color insert, plus b/w photos, Quality PB, 978-1-59473-216-4 **$18.99**

The Soulwork of Clay: A Hands-On Approach to Spirituality
by Marjory Zoet Bankson; Photos by Peter Bankson
Takes you through the seven-step process of making clay into a pot, drawing parallels at each stage to the process of spiritual growth.
7 × 9, 192 pp, b/w photos, Quality PB, 978-1-59473-249-2 **$16.99**

Kabbalah / Enneagram
(Books from Jewish Lights Publishing, SkyLight Paths' sister imprint)

Cast in God's Image: Discover Your Personality Type Using the Enneagram and Kabbalah
by Rabbi Howard A. Addison, PhD 7 × 9, 176 pp, Quality PB, 978-1-58023-124-4 **$16.95**

Ehyeh: A Kabbalah for Tomorrow *by Rabbi Arthur Green, PhD*
6 × 9, 224 pp, Quality PB, 978-1-58023-213-5 **$18.99**

The Enneagram and Kabbalah, 2nd Edition: Reading Your Soul
by Rabbi Howard A. Addison, PhD 6 × 9, 192 pp, Quality PB, 978-1-58023-229-6 **$16.99**

The Gift of Kabbalah: Discovering the Secrets of Heaven, Renewing Your Life on Earth
by Tamar Frankiel, PhD 6 × 9, 256 pp, Quality PB, 978-1-58023-141-1 **$16.95**

God in Your Body: Kabbalah, Mindfulness and Embodied Spiritual Practice
by Jay Michaelson 6 × 9, 272 pp, Quality PB, 978-1-58023-304-0 **$18.99**

Jewish Mysticism and the Spiritual Life: Classical Texts, Contemporary Reflections
Edited by Dr. Lawrence Fine, Dr. Eitan Fishbane and Rabbi Or N. Rose
6 × 9, 256 pp, HC, 978-1-58023-434-4 **$24.99**

Kabbalah: A Brief Introduction for Christians
by Tamar Frankiel, PhD 5½ × 8¼, 208 pp, Quality PB, 978-1-58023-303-3 **$16.99**

Zohar: Annotated & Explained *Translation & Annotation by Daniel C. Matt;*
Foreword by Andrew Harvey 5½ × 8¼, 176 pp, Quality PB, 978-1-893361-51-5 **$15.99**

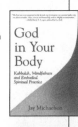

Spiritual Practice

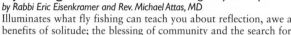

Fly Fishing—The Sacred Art: Casting a Fly as a Spiritual Practice
by Rabbi Eric Eisenkramer and Rev. Michael Attas, MD
Illuminates what fly fishing can teach you about reflection, awe and wonder; the benefits of solitude; the blessing of community and the search for the Divine.
5½ x 8½, 192 pp (est), Quality PB, 978-1-59473-299-7 **$16.99**

Lectio Divina—**The Sacred Art:** Transforming Words & Images into Heart-Centered Prayer *by Christine Valters Paintner, PhD*
Expands the practice of sacred reading beyond scriptural texts and makes it accessible in contemporary life. 5½ x 8½, 240 pp, Quality PB, 978-1-59473-300-0 **$16.99**

Haiku—The Sacred Art: A Spiritual Practice in Three Lines
by Margaret D. McGee 5½ x 8½, 192 pp, Quality PB, 978-1-59473-269-0 **$16.99**

Dance—The Sacred Art: The Joy of Movement as a Spiritual Practice
by Cynthia Winton-Henry 5½ x 8½, 224 pp, Quality PB, 978-1-59473-268-3 **$16.99**

Spiritual Adventures in the Snow: Skiing & Snowboarding as Renewal for Your Soul *by Dr. Marcia McFee and Rev. Karen Foster; Foreword by Paul Arthur*
5½ x 8½, 208 pp, Quality PB, 978-1-59473-270-6 **$16.99**

Divining the Body: Reclaim the Holiness of Your Physical Self *by Jan Phillips*
8 x 8, 256 pp, Quality PB, 978-1-59473-080-1 **$16.99**

Everyday Herbs in Spiritual Life: A Guide to Many Practices
by Michael J. Caduto; Foreword by Rosemary Gladstar
7 x 9, 208 pp, 20+ b/w illus., Quality PB, 978-1-59473-174-7 **$16.99**

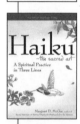

Giving—The Sacred Art: Creating a Lifestyle of Generosity
by Lauren Tyler Wright 5½ x 8½, 208 pp, Quality PB, 978-1-59473-224-9 **$16.99**

Hospitality—The Sacred Art: Discovering the Hidden Spiritual Power of Invitation and Welcome *by Rev. Nanette Sawyer; Foreword by Rev. Dirk Ficca*
5½ x 8½, 208 pp, Quality PB, 978-1-59473-228-7 **$16.99**

Labyrinths from the Outside In: Walking to Spiritual Insight—A Beginner's Guide
by Donna Schaper and Carole Ann Camp
6 x 9, 208 pp, b/w illus. and photos, Quality PB, 978-1-893361-18-8 **$16.95**

Practicing the Sacred Art of Listening: A Guide to Enrich Your Relationships and Kindle Your Spiritual Life *by Kay Lindahl* 8 x 8, 176 pp, Quality PB, 978-1-893361-85-0 **$16.95**

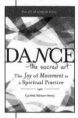

Recovery—The Sacred Art: The Twelve Steps as Spiritual Practice *by Rami Shapiro; Foreword by Joan Borysenko, PhD* 5½ x 8½, 240 pp, Quality PB, 978-1-59473-259-1 **$16.99**

Running—The Sacred Art: Preparing to Practice *by Dr. Warren A. Kay; Foreword by Kristin Armstrong* 5½ x 8½, 160 pp, Quality PB, 978-1-59473-227-0 **$16.99**

The Sacred Art of Chant: Preparing to Practice
by Ana Hernández 5½ x 8½, 192 pp, Quality PB, 978-1-59473-036-8 **$15.99**

The Sacred Art of Fasting: Preparing to Practice
by Thomas Ryan, CSP 5½ x 8½, 192 pp, Quality PB, 978-1-59473-078-8 **$15.99**

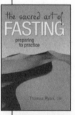

The Sacred Art of Forgiveness: Forgiving Ourselves and Others through God's Grace
by Marcia Ford 8 x 8, 176 pp, Quality PB, 978-1-59473-175-4 **$18.99**

The Sacred Art of Listening: Forty Reflections for Cultivating a Spiritual Practice
by Kay Lindahl; Illus. by Amy Schnapper 8 x 8, 160 pp, b/w illus., Quality PB, 978-1-893361-44-7 **$16.99**

The Sacred Art of Lovingkindness: Preparing to Practice
by Rabbi Rami Shapiro; Foreword by Marcia Ford 5½ x 8½, 176 pp, Quality PB, 978-1-59473-151-8 **$16.99**

Sacred Attention: A Spiritual Practice for Finding God in the Moment
by Margaret D. McGee 6 x 9, 144 pp, Quality PB, 978-1-59473-291-1 **$16.99**

Soul Fire: Accessing Your Creativity
by Thomas Ryan, CSP 6 x 9, 160 pp, Quality PB, 978-1-59473-243-0 **$16.99**

Thanking & Blessing—The Sacred Art: Spiritual Vitality through Gratefulness
by Jay Marshall, PhD; Foreword by Philip Gulley 5½ x 8½, 176 pp, Quality PB, 978-1-59473-231-7 **$16.99**

Spiritual Poetry—The Mystic Poets

Experience these mystic poets as you never have before. Each beautiful, compact book includes a brief introduction to the poet's time and place, a summary of the major themes of the poet's mysticism and religious tradition, essential selections from the poet's most important works, and an appreciative preface by a contemporary spiritual writer.

Hafiz
The Mystic Poets
Translated and with Notes by Gertrude Bell
Preface by Ibrahim Gamard

Hafiz is known throughout the world as Persia's greatest poet, with sales of his poems in Iran today only surpassed by those of the Qur'an itself. His probing and joyful verse speaks to people from all backgrounds who long to taste and feel divine love and experience harmony with all living things.
5 x 7¼, 144 pp, HC, 978-1-59473-009-2 **$16.99**

Hopkins
The Mystic Poets
Preface by Rev. Thomas Ryan, CSP

Gerard Manley Hopkins, Christian mystical poet, is beloved for his use of fresh language and startling metaphors to describe the world around him. Although his verse is lovely, beneath the surface lies a searching soul, wrestling with and yearning for God.
5 x 7¼, 112 pp, HC, 978-1-59473-010-8 **$16.99**

Tagore
The Mystic Poets
Preface by Swami Adiswarananda

Rabindranath Tagore is often considered the Shakespeare of modern India. A great mystic, Tagore was the teacher of W. B. Yeats and Robert Frost, the close friend of Albert Einstein and Mahatma Gandhi, and the winner of the Nobel Prize for Literature. This beautiful sampling of Tagore's two most important works, *The Gardener* and *Gitanjali,* offers a glimpse into his spiritual vision that has inspired people around the world.
5 x 7¼, 144 pp, HC, 978-1-59473-008-5 **$16.99**

Whitman
The Mystic Poets
Preface by Gary David Comstock

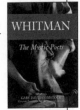

Walt Whitman was the most innovative and influential poet of the nineteenth century. This beautiful sampling of Whitman's most important poetry from *Leaves of Grass,* and selections from his prose writings, offers a glimpse into the spiritual side of his most radical themes—love for country, love for others and love of self.
5 x 7¼, 192 pp, HC, 978-1-59473-041-2 **$16.99**

Prayer / Meditation

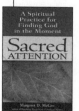

Sacred Attention: A Spiritual Practice for Finding God in the Moment
by Margaret D. McGee
Framed on the Christian liturgical year, this inspiring guide explores ways to develop a practice of attention as a means of talking—and listening—to God.
6 x 9, 144 pp, Quality PB, 978-1-59473-291-1 **$16.99**

Women of Color Pray: Voices of Strength, Faith, Healing, Hope and Courage
Edited and with Introductions by Christal M. Jackson
Through these prayers, poetry, lyrics, meditations and affirmations, you will share in the strong and undeniable connection women of color share with God.
5 x 7¼, 208 pp, Quality PB, 978-1-59473-077-1 **$15.99**

Secrets of Prayer: A Multifaith Guide to Creating Personal Prayer in Your Life *by Nancy Corcoran, CSJ*
This compelling, multifaith guidebook offers you companionship and encouragement on the journey to a healthy prayer life. 6 x 9, 160 pp, Quality PB, 978-1-59473-215-7 **$16.99**

Prayers to an Evolutionary God
by William Cleary; Afterword by Diarmuid O'Murchu
Inspired by the spiritual and scientific teachings of Diarmuid O'Murchu and Teilhard de Chardin, reveals that religion and science can be combined to create an expanding view of the universe—an evolutionary faith.
6 x 9, 208 pp, HC, 978-1-59473-006-1 **$21.99**

The Art of Public Prayer, 2nd Edition: Not for Clergy Only
by Lawrence A. Hoffman, PhD 6 x 9, 288 pp, Quality PB, 978-1-893361-06-5 **$19.99**

A Heart of Stillness: A Complete Guide to Learning the Art of Meditation
by David A. Cooper 5½ x 8½, 272 pp, Quality PB, 978-1-893361-03-4 **$18.99**

Meditation without Gurus: A Guide to the Heart of Practice
by Clark Strand 5½ x 8½, 192 pp, Quality PB, 978-1-893361-93-5 **$16.95**

Praying with Our Hands: 21 Practices of Embodied Prayer from the World's Spiritual Traditions *by Jon M. Sweeney; Photos by Jennifer J. Wilson; Foreword by Mother Tessa Bielecki; Afterword by Taitetsu Unno, PhD*
8 x 8, 96 pp, 22 duotone photos, Quality PB, 978-1-893361-16-4 **$16.95**

Three Gates to Meditation Practice: A Personal Journey into Sufism, Buddhism, and Judaism *by David A. Cooper* 5½ x 8½, 240 pp, Quality PB, 978-1-893361-22-5 **$16.95**

Prayer / M. Basil Pennington, OCSO

Finding Grace at the Center, 3rd Edition: The Beginning of Centering Prayer *with Thomas Keating, OCSO, and Thomas E. Clarke, SJ; Foreword by Rev. Cynthia Bourgeault, PhD* A practical guide to a simple and beautiful form of meditative prayer. 5 x 7¼, 128 pp, Quality PB, 978-1-59473-182-2 **$12.99**

The Monks of Mount Athos: A Western Monk's Extraordinary Spiritual Journey on Eastern Holy Ground *Foreword by Archimandrite Dionysios*
Explores the landscape, monastic communities and food of Athos.
6 x 9, 352 pp, Quality PB, 978-1-893361-78-2 **$18.95**

Psalms: A Spiritual Commentary *Illus. by Phillip Ratner*
Reflections on some of the most beloved passages from the Bible's most widely read book. 6 x 9, 176 pp, 24 full-page b/w illus., Quality PB, 978-1-59473-234-8 **$16.99**

The Song of Songs: A Spiritual Commentary *Illus. by Phillip Ratner*
Explore the Bible's most challenging mystical text.
6 x 9, 160 pp, 14 full-page b/w illus., Quality PB, 978-1-59473-235-5 **$16.99**
HC, 978-1-59473-004-7 **$19.99**

Women's Interest

Spiritually Healthy Divorce: Navigating Disruption with Insight & Hope
by Carolyne Call
A spiritual map to help you move through the twists and turns of divorce.
6 x 9, 224 pp, Quality PB, 978-1-59473-288-1 **$16.99**

New Feminist Christianity: Many Voices, Many Views
Edited by Mary E. Hunt and Diann L. Neu
Insights from ministers and theologians, activists and leaders, artists and liturgists who are shaping the future. Taken together, their voices offer a starting point for building new models of religious life and worship.
6 x 9, 384 pp, HC, 978-1-59473-285-0 **$24.99**

New Jewish Feminism: Probing the Past, Forging the Future
Edited by Rabbi Elyse Goldstein; Foreword by Anita Diamant
Looks at the growth and accomplishments of Jewish feminism and what they mean for Jewish women today and tomorrow. Features the voices of women from every area of Jewish life, addressing the important issues that concern Jewish women.
6 x 9, 480 pp, Quality PB, 978-1-58023-448-1 **$19.99**; HC, 978-1-58023-359-0 **$24.99***

Bread, Body, Spirit: Finding the Sacred in Food
Edited and with Introductions by Alice Peck
6 x 9, 224 pp, Quality PB, 978-1-59473-242-3 **$19.99**

Dance—The Sacred Art: The Joy of Movement as a Spiritual Practice
by Cynthia Winton-Henry 5½ x 8½, 224 pp, Quality PB, 978-1-59473-268-3 **$16.99**

Daughters of the Desert: Stories of Remarkable Women from Christian, Jewish and Muslim Traditions
by Claire Rudolf Murphy, Meghan Nuttall Sayres, Mary Cronk Farrell, Sarah Conover and Betsy Wharton
5½ x 8½, 192 pp, Illus., Quality PB, 978-1-59473-106-8 **$14.99** Inc. reader's discussion guide

The Divine Feminine in Biblical Wisdom Literature
Selections Annotated & Explained
Translation & Annotation by Rabbi Rami Shapiro; Foreword by Rev. Cynthia Bourgeault, PhD
5½ x 8½, 240 pp, Quality PB, 978-1-59473-109-9 **$16.99**

Divining the Body: Reclaim the Holiness of Your Physical Self
by Jan Phillips 8 x 8, 256 pp, Quality PB, 978-1-59473-080-1 **$16.99**

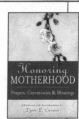

Honoring Motherhood: Prayers, Ceremonies & Blessings
Edited and with Introductions by Lynn L Caruso 5 x 7¼, 272 pp, HC, 978-1-59473-239-3 **$19.99**

Next to Godliness: Finding the Sacred in Housekeeping
Edited by Alice Peck 6 x 9, 224 pp, Quality PB, 978-1-59473-214-0 **$19.99**

ReVisions: Seeing Torah through a Feminist Lens
by Rabbi Elyse Goldstein 5½ x 8½, 224 pp, Quality PB, 978-1-58023-117-6 **$16.95***

The Triumph of Eve & Other Subversive Bible Tales
by Matt Biers-Ariel 5½ x 8½, 192 pp, Quality PB, 978-1-59473-176-1 **$14.99**

White Fire: A Portrait of Women Spiritual Leaders in America
by Malka Drucker; Photos by Gay Block 7 x 10, 320 pp, b/w photos, HC, 978-1-893361-64-5 **$24.95**

Woman Spirit Awakening in Nature
Growing Into the Fullness of Who You Are
by Nancy Barrett Chickerneo, PhD; Foreword by Eileen Fisher
8 x 8, 224 pp, b/w illus., Quality PB, 978-1-59473-250-8 **$16.99**

Women of Color Pray: Voices of Strength, Faith, Healing, Hope and Courage
Edited and with Introductions by Christal M. Jackson
5 x 7¼, 208 pp, Quality PB, 978-1-59473-077-1 **$15.99**

The Women's Torah Commentary: New Insights from Women Rabbis on the 54 Weekly Torah Portions *Edited by Rabbi Elyse Goldstein*
6 x 9, 496 pp, Quality PB, 978-1-58023-370-5 **$19.99**; HC, 978-1-58023-076-6 **$34.95***

* A book from Jewish Lights, SkyLight Paths' sister imprint

About SKYLIGHT PATHS Publishing

SkyLight Paths Publishing is creating a place where people of different spiritual traditions come together for challenge and inspiration, a place where we can help each other understand the mystery that lies at the heart of our existence.

Through spirituality, our religious beliefs are increasingly becoming a part of our lives—rather than *apart* from our lives. While many of us may be more interested than ever in spiritual growth, we may be less firmly planted in traditional religion. Yet, we do want to deepen our relationship to the sacred, to learn from our own as well as from other faith traditions, and to practice in new ways.

SkyLight Paths sees both believers and seekers as a community that increasingly transcends traditional boundaries of religion and denomination—people wanting to learn from each other, *walking together, finding the way.*

For your information and convenience, at the back of this book we have provided a list of other SkyLight Paths books you might find interesting and useful. They cover the following subjects:

Buddhism / Zen	Global Spiritual	Monasticism
Catholicism	Perspectives	Mysticism
Children's Books	Gnosticism	Poetry
Christianity	Hinduism /	Prayer
Comparative	Vedanta	Religious Etiquette
Religion	Inspiration	Retirement
Current Events	Islam / Sufism	Spiritual Biography
Earth-Based	Judaism	Spiritual Direction
Spirituality	Kabbalah	Spirituality
Enneagram	Meditation	Women's Interest
	Midrash Fiction	Worship

Or phone, fax, mail or e-mail to: SKYLIGHT PATHS Publishing
Sunset Farm Offices, Route 4 • P.O. Box 237 • Woodstock, Vermont 05091
Tel: (802) 457-4000 • Fax: (802) 457-4004 • www.skylightpaths.com
Credit card orders: (800) 962-4544 (8:30AM–5:30PM ET Monday–Friday)
Generous discounts on quantity orders. SATISFACTION GUARANTEED. Prices subject to change.